W9-BUK-483

<u>Top Leaders and Professionals Share Advance Praise for...</u>

The Power of Meeting New People

Debra Fine

"In our business, casual conversation is an essential leadership skill. Demonstrating conversational skills and techniques that build rapport and relationships in both social and business situations is a key to success."

—Vice President, People Development, AMERUS Group

"All the information Debra Fine discusses can be used in personal life, as well as professional life."

—Texas Dental Association

"I realize from your material that 'casual conversation' is a valid component of my job and of everyone's life. Casual conversation is a pleasure if you make it one, and trivial only if you think connecting with other human beings is trivial."

**—Dan Underwood, Vail
Ski Resort**

"Your message is sure to not only be reflected in improved customer service but also in people suddenly volunteering to go to the next corporate 'mixer.'"

—General Manager, Destination Services of Colorado, Inc.

The Power of Meeting New People

Start Conversations, Keep Them Going,
Build Rapport, Develop
Friendships, and Expand Business

Debra Fine

A Possibility Press Book

The Power of Meeting New People

Debra Fine

Copyright © 2005 by Debra Fine
ISBN 0-938716-52-2

1   2   3   4   5   6   7   8   9   10

Published by
Possibility Press
possibilitypress@aol.com

Manufactured in the United States of America

Dedication

Dedicated with love to the
wind beneath my wings, my husband Steve,
and my two magnificent sources of
inspiration, Jared and Sarah.

"...The People You Meet."

As I've been known to say, "You're the same today as you'll be in five years except for the books you read and the people you meet." Now here's a tremendous book that teaches you how to rev up your ability to meet new people. It'll help you supercharge your business or career, and energize all areas of your life.

Debra Fine teaches us how to expand the number of people we meet so we can excel at whatever we are doing. Everyone I know who is extraordinarily successful has met lots of people. But it's not the people you know that counts. It's the people who know _you_ and how you can help them with what you have to offer that determines your success.

The Power of Meeting New People is jam packed with must-read information and examples that can help you meet more people and have great fun doing it. Read this book and blow your people-meeting skills through the roof. You, too, will then be on your way to even more tremendous success.

Tremendously,

Charlie "Tremendous" Jones

Contents

"Start thinking of strangers as future friends—not as people to be feared or avoided. After all, our friends and associates were once strangers. Meeting new people and becoming a good conversationalist will help you bring new people into your network of associates, friends, colleagues, clients, customers, and others."

—Debra Fine

If I Can Do It, So Can You

"There is no doubt that meeting new people and enhancing your conversational skills will improve your life."
—Debra Fine—

When I first got into the business of helping others meet new people and cultivate conversational skills, I ran into a lot of skepticism. Executives scoffed at the idea as a housewife's trivial initiative to overcome boredom. Then I would get clandestine calls for assistance from folks with prestigious titles. They would construct elaborate covert operations to seek advice without admitting their true agendas. As it turned out, people were actually embarrassed about it, and I can appreciate that.

In my previous life as a nerdy engineer, I was burdened by poor social skills and embarrassed by my own conversational ineptitude. Before I gave myself a remedial education in the power of meeting new people, I had been a poor communicator and a timid person for as long as I can recall.

As a kid I was overweight and reticent—invisible in the back of the class, and often excluded because of my size. One of the most vivid memories of my childhood is that of a birthday party for my third-grade classmate, Rita. All the girls in my class were invited except one other girl and me. I felt so hurt that I withdrew into a world of books. I had no idea how to make a friend or have a friend. Consequently, I never learned how to talk to my peers.

Little Chatting Was Required and No New Friends Were Necessary

Naturally, when I got older, I selected a career that didn't have a high demand for meeting new people. Engineering was the perfect choice for me since it tends to be highly technical and requires little chatting. I routinely made technical presentations or answered complex engineering questions without any trouble. All that was required was technical competence in my field. However, as my career progressed, I was sent to conferences and industry meetings where I was expected to mingle with colleagues, network, and meet clients. This struck fear into my heart.

I only knew one way to introduce myself and start a conversation. Without fail, I would ask every person I met, "What do you do?" After we exchanged career notes, the conversation invariably sputtered to an agonizing halt. I just didn't know how to keep it going. As a result, I skipped every social function I could. For the ones I couldn't avoid, I'd go late and leave early. In-between I'd pray that some other dear souls with better skills and a kind heart would rescue me by introducing themselves and initiating a conversation.

I struggled with the art of meeting new people and starting conversations throughout my tenure as an engineer. Then I took a break from my career to have my two children. During that interlude, I began feeling the need to have more friends so that I could expand my horizons. To do so, I knew that I had to improve my social and relationship-building skills. So, I began taking note of others who were successful at mingling and cultivating friendships in crowds. I watched what they did and timidly began trying to imitate them.

Meeting New People Is Not Rocket Science

Here I was approaching 40, having been out of my field for several years, and needing to meet people to further my career once my children became old enough. It was a daunting prospect, to say the least. Nevertheless, I realized that acquiring people-meeting and conversational skills couldn't be anywhere near as complicated as rocket science. I easily convinced myself that it couldn't be that tough, because I had observed so many other people of various backgrounds doing it well. So I made it my goal to figure out how to start and keep a conversation going for longer than five minutes.

I soon discovered that a key element to meeting new people is *casual conversation.* I finally understood what a great tool it was for building rapport. I devoted myself to learning more about it, practicing it, and helping others become good at it. Ever since I started my speaking and consulting business, I have been devoted to helping others develop the power of meeting new people. I have met countless fascinating people, made many wonderful friends, and I now have a continuous stream of business referrals. My life is richly populated with diverse individuals who bring added meaning and depth to each day.

My goal in writing this book is to offer what I've learned so that you, too, can reap the tremendous rewards that come from meeting new people and having a repertoire of conversational skills. The tips and techniques in this book are for everyone— not just nerds!

The Conversationally Challenged Are Not Alone

I know salespeople who are wonderful at making formal presentations, but they enter networking events in a cold sweat. There are teachers who can chat with students and colleagues; but when they see parents at school functions, they don't have the slightest idea what to say. There are harried, yet happy, stay-at-home moms who are bundles of entertainment at playgroups, yet they walk away from community organization meetings or events at their places of worship feeling isolated and disconnected.

I know a fine physician who closed his practice and joined an HMO (Health Maintenance Organization) because, despite his expertise, he didn't have the conversational skills and confidence to garner new referrals. There are many business owners and other professionals whose success depends on their ability to network with others, yet they fail to grow their businesses or professions because they are afraid of meeting new people and starting conversations. I've found that there are an incredible number of perfectly competent people, from all walks of life, who need help in acquiring the ability and harnessing their power to meet new people and develop conversational skills. So if you are among them, you are certainly not alone!

Expand Your Horizons—*Meet Some New People*

This book will help you acquire the skills you need to meet new people and enhance your conversational abilities. As your skills grow, the quality of your life will improve. Becoming a good conversationalist has an amazing ripple effect. It will help you bring new people into your network of associates, friends, colleagues, clients, customers, and others. You will get joy out of events you used to dread, and you'll create pathways and channels for opportunities to meet more new people.

Now take a moment and invest some time considering the following statements. If you check yes to most of them, you are on the right track. If you find yourself responding no to more than a couple, it's time to get to work.

Developing the Power of Meeting New People

Check Yes or No to the following statements:

1. I have joined or participated in at least one club, group, or other activity in order to meet new people for business or personal reasons. ___ Yes ___ No

2. I'm conscious of taking turns sharing in conversations so I can get to know others and help them get to know me. ___ Yes ___ No

3. I have helped at least two people meet potential associates, customers, or clients in order to assist them in their networking skills. ___ Yes ___ No

4. I have attended at least two functions, events, or activities a month where I can meet people who are either decision makers or potential new friends. ___ Yes ___ No

5. If someone is friendly toward me it is easy to be friendly back. However, I don't wait to make sure someone is friendly before I am friendly toward him or her. I initiate the friendly gesture. ___ Yes ___ No

6. When someone asks me "What's new?" instead of saying "Not much," I talk about something exciting.
___Yes ___No

7. At meetings, parties, and virtually everywhere I go, I introduce myself to people I don't know and come away knowing the names and having the contact information of at least three people. ___Yes ___No

Well, how did you do? All right, that's enough casual conversation. Now let's get down to business!

"Becoming a good conversationalist has an amazing ripple effect. You will get joy out of events you used to dread, and you'll create pathways and channels for opportunities to meet more new people."

—Debra Fine

"The great news about the skills needed to meet and engage in conversations with new people is that anyone can learn them. While some people have more of a tendency to be effective meeters and greeters, most have had to work at it."

—Debra Fine

-1-

So What's the Big Deal About Meeting New People?

"People who excel at meeting new people are actually experts at making others feel included, valued, and comfortable."
—Debra Fine—

Jack pulls into the parking lot, turns off the engine, and sits for a minute, dreading the next two hours. An important client has invited him to an open house in celebration of opening a new downtown office.

Jack hates these things—he never knows what to say, won't know anyone except the client, and will feel nervous while trying not to look lost. So he always eats more than he knows is good for him, just to keep occupied.

Jack needs to attend—that's a given—but he sinks deeper into the front seat and agonizes over how long he'll have to stay. Is dropping by for 30 minutes enough, or will he insult one of his best clients if he doesn't stay for the whole event? He searches for excuses to get himself out of there early. He could have someone page him at a specified time and use that as an excuse for a quick exit...perhaps one of the kids has a big game...or maybe he just allows his anxiety to carry him right into an illness. Does any of this sound familiar?

Gear Up for More Enjoyable Daily Interactions

Typically, casual conversations can occur at least a dozen times a day—on the way into work, picking up your child from an after-school activity, riding the elevator with a colleague, fielding a phone call from your mother-in-law, attending an industry meeting, taking a client or associate to lunch, going to a job interview, sharing an opportunity, product, or service with a prospect—the list is endless!

But for many of us, the demands for meeting new people don't ever make it any easier. If anything, such encounters may increase anxiety and cause some people to fear or even avoid going to social events or business lunches, and risking chance encounters with neighbors or others.

Do your conversations evaporate almost as soon as they've begun? Are you a reluctant participant at social or business get-togethers? If so, this book will help you attain the conversational skills you need to feel confident and poised in *any* situation. When you practice the simple techniques and approaches shown, you will put your meeting-new-people demons behind you. You will learn how to:

- Engage anyone in a meaningful dialogue.
- Rejuvenate a dying conversation.
- Transition into new topics.
- Feel more at ease at networking events, parties, and receptions.
- Develop business friendships.
- Step out of a conversation with grace.

Getting to the BIG Stuff

Casual conversation is often thought of as the lowly stepchild of real conversation, yet it serves an extremely important function. Without it, you can rarely get to the real conversation. Casual conversation is the icebreaker—your first comment or question upon meeting a new person—that clears the way for more in-depth conversations and stronger relationships. People who excel at casual conversation are actually experts at making others feel included, valued, and comfortable. And that goes a long way toward furthering business relationships, closing deals, and making new friends and associations.

The great news about the skills needed to meet and engage in conversations with new people is that anyone can learn them. Don't be fooled into thinking that all those other people you see who are smiling and happily mingling came by it naturally. While some have more of a tendency to be effective meeters and greeters, most have had to work at it. They've practiced, attended seminars, received guidance from coaches or other leaders, listened to tapes, and read books. Don't think so? Trust me, I know. I used to be a geeky, introverted engineer—no one has worse skills than I once did. But I became a pro by learning the skills and then practicing them. It was that simple.

The first step in obtaining success is letting go of the idea that we all are somehow supposed to know how to meet and converse with people we don't know or hardly know. It's simply not true. We are rarely taught how to do it, nor is there some biological mechanism that instinctively takes over when we find ourselves with a conversational opportunity.

Mark McCormack, an attorney from Cleveland who founded one of the first sports management firms in the United States said, "All things being equal, people will buy from a friend. All things being not quite so equal, people will still buy from a friend." The bottom line is that it's to your benefit to cultivate friendships, not just collect business cards.

In his book *Megatrends,* John Naisbitt discussed our need for high-touch in our high-tech world: "The more technology around us, the more need for human touch." People are compensating for living in a high-tech world of computers, e-mail, and being alone in work settings by reaching out to other people. Witness the fact that shopping malls are some of the most frequented places in the world! People need to gather—to connect and have caring relationships. When you make the extra effort to meet new people, you are extending the hand of friendship that is usually warmly received.

Talk Is Cheap—*But It Can Be Quite Valuable*

Casual conversation is essential in creating and enhancing business relationships. Always begin and end a business talk with casual conversation. For example, people choose financial planners as much for their ability to help them *feel* secure and comfortable personally as they do for their financial savvy. How important is your physician's "bedside manner" to you? Hair stylists are often consummate conversationalists. They understand that few people will spend the better part of an hour or more, sitting in a chair at the mercy of someone with a sharp instrument, unless he or she feels comfortable with that person!

In an indirect but very important way, casual conversation is related to how businesses and individuals spend or invest time and money:

- **To get their problems solved or their wants or needs met.** Think about it—you may dash into a fast food restaurant for lunch to avoid packing leftovers. You might hire a babysitter to have an evening out. You may pay someone to cut your grass so that you can have more time to invest meeting potential prospects or more free time.

- **To gain good, positive feelings.** My neighbor Susan continues banking with the same institution she has for years—even though another bank offered a better free-checking deal—because she likes the people. My friend Vince moved to the opposite side of town and still drives back to the old neighborhood to take his dog to the vet. Although he and the vet do not socialize together, he can't imagine going anywhere else. He likes that particular vet. (Hopefully his dog does too!)

A good conversationalist frequently gives the positive attention necessary to stimulate the good feelings people long to have. The reality is that people's choices about those with whom they choose to associate and where to spend their money are influenced by the presence or absence of rapport—a harmonious, empathetic connection. Casual conversation is a big deal because it is integral to establishing this precious rapport. Parents and teachers visit before conferences to create bonds. Mortgage brokers chat with people at referral sources, like title and real estate companies, to strengthen their relationships which will lead to more business.

It's a challenging and fast-paced world, and the news media provides more bad news than good. People appreciate conversations in which they feel acknowledged, heard, and significant. While it's understood that people seek these benefits in conversations with friends, it's also true that people choose to associate in business with and buy goods and services from individuals who are warm, friendly, and caring. From the senior executives of a large corporation seeking a supplier, to a parent picking up a few groceries, to the account executive in need of a courier—buying decisions are all influenced by the rapport, or lack of it, established with the other party.

Garner BIG Gains—*With a Little Talking*

Effective managers and other leaders use casual conversation at the front end of meetings to set the mood for discussion and create a bridge to more meaningful, and perhaps difficult, dialogue. Casual conversations and formal icebreakers offer opportunities to build rapport, increase success, and create cohesive teams.

By developing more casual conversational skills, you can even improve communication with your children. You'll recognize the most repeated question in parenting—"How was school?"—as a conversation killer. You can avoid the usual one-word response—"Fine"—and create a meaningful dialogue. Imagine being able to gain valuable insights about what they're learning and who their friends are!

Casual conversation is no small thing. It's a precious personal and professional tool you can use to connect with other people. Appreciating the power of casual conversation is the first step. By recognizing its value, you'll be more inclined to put forth the effort necessary to acquire the skills. If you thought casual conversation was all about becoming a smooth-talker to take advantage of people, you were misinformed. It's more like that first domino; it causes a positive chain reaction with all kinds of implications for more success in all areas of your life.

This book is filled with tips and techniques to help you develop the skills you need to meet new people and enjoy the perks of quality conversations. You may even decide that you love attending networking events, parties, and meeting people everywhere you go because you will have the skills to be more successful with them.

Like me, you may still prefer to stay at home with a good book rather than attend an event at which you don't know anyone—*but you'll go anyway*. There's no denying that it takes effort to mingle when a room is full of people you don't know. However, there's also no denying that there are plenty of times all of us need to attend such events as a part of our jobs, businesses, or personal lives. So it just makes sense to maximize those opportunities. Improved people-meeting and casual conversational skills offer you the tools to do just that.

By the time you've finished this book you'll have the information and resources you need to be a successful conversationalist anywhere you see people. Upgrading your casual conversational skills can enhance your leadership abilities, reduce your anxiety in social situations, boost your confidence, lead to new friendships and business relationships, and more. Before you know it, you will actually look forward to and enjoy meeting and talking to people you don't know.

"*Silence is not always golden—it can be impolite and hold you back. The old adage that says silence is golden can be detrimental to your success.*"

—DebraFine

-2-

Get Over Your Parents' Good Intentions

"Waiting will net you a bunch of lost time.
You need to take the initiative. Don't spend another
minute thinking that if you just keep waiting, interesting
people will introduce themselves to you."
—Debra Fine—

It's no wonder so many of us have trouble with our people-meeting and conversational skills. Some of our childhood memories may still haunt and influence us as adults, predisposing us to refrain from introducing ourselves and initiating conversations. When we were impressionable toddlers, many of our parents taught us:

- Good things come to those who wait.
- Silence is golden.
- Wait to be properly introduced.
- Don't talk to strangers.

Those messages served us well as kids; the advice helped ensure our safety and taught us manners. But now, as adults, our safety isn't at stake with every new person we meet. And by now, our manners are well established. The time has come to replace those old messages with more relevant advice, and here it is.

In Safe Situations—*Always Talk to Strangers*

To expand your circle of friends, associates, colleagues, clients, or customers you need to start engaging strangers and acquaintances in conversations. There's just no way around it. Strangers have the potential to become good friends, long-term clients or customers, valued associates, and bridges to new experiences and other people. Start thinking of strangers as people who can bring new dimensions into your life and vice versa—not as persons to be feared or avoided. Remember, all of our friends and associates were once strangers!

Take the Initiative—*Smile, Say Hello, and Introduce Yourself First*

When was the last time someone properly introduced you to another person? The truth is that the host of a gathering rarely takes the time to do so in a meaningful way. You've probably been to this kind of event. You go to a holiday open house. The host or hostess greets you, takes your coat, visits for a moment, and shows you to the food. He or she departs to greet another guest and you are left standing next to the shrimp cocktail, not knowing anyone in the room. If you wait for the host to come back and properly introduce you to some of the other guests, chances are your only new encounter will be with the shrimp.

Times have changed. People expect you to mingle on your own, introduce yourself, and take the initiative to get acquainted. As Babe Ruth said, "Don't let the fear of striking out get in your way." Remember, even your closest confidante was once a stranger. Take the risk. Smile, walk up to someone and introduce yourself. Extend the hand of friend-

ship, make eye contact, and smile saying, "Hello. My name is
_____. It's nice to meet you."

Whether or not you are a member of an association, chamber of commerce, fraternity or sorority, or place of worship, you are probably aware of those organizations' constant challenges of retaining and increasing memberships. We join the organizations seeking fellowship or business connections; but we often leave or quit if we don't find what we want. Instead, we may perceive others as groups of cliques that we are incapable of joining. I think most of us can relate to the following poem, author unknown:

Thoughts From a New Member

I see you at the meetings, but you never say hello.
You're busy all the time you're there
With those you really know.
I sit among the members; yet I'm a lonely gal.
The new ones feel as strange as I; the old ones pass us by.
Darn it, you folks urged us to join and talked of fellowship.
You could just cross the room, you know;
But you never make the trip.
Can't you just nod your head and smile
Or stop and shake a hand,
Then go sit among your friends?
Now that I'd understand.
I'll be at your next meeting, and hope that you will spend
The time to introduce yourself; I joined to be your friend.

Look around the room at your next opportunity to spend time at a reception, coffee break, hospitality room, wedding, or other function. Find the person who looks approachable to you and engage him or her in conversation. And remember the line in the tune that says "When you're smiling, the whole world smiles at you."

Silence Is *Not* Always Golden—*It Can Be Impolite and Hold You Back*

Strict adherence to the old adage that says "silence is golden" can be detrimental to your success. My first realization of the downside of silence came when I was an engineer working side by side with a peer who had the same academic credentials, tenure, and work quality as mine. We were considered technical equals in the best sense of the word. However, she was outgoing and conversational. Staff members in marketing, human resources, and quality control, and many executives at corporate headquarters as well, knew her. Even our immediate supervisor noticed her, and frequently commented on her work. When it came time for a promotion, she got it—I didn't. I just wasn't as visible because I was so silent.

I later learned another costly lesson about silence. My friend, Johnnie, a regional director with a *Fortune 100* company, dragged me to all her company functions. Her boss, Bob, a senior vice president, attended those functions too. I admired his presence, poise, and graciousness as he easily conversed with everyone. Bob's self-confidence intimidated me so much that I rarely talked with him, despite my respect for him. Even when he approached me, I was too nervous to say much.

When I moved into engineering sales, I called on Bob to reintroduce myself and promote my employer's services. But before I could even finish my introduction, Bob blasted me, saying, "I can't believe you're calling on me. We've been at the same parties a dozen times, and you've ignored me at every one. You're the biggest snob I know. I have no interest in buying anything from you."

Needless to say, I was stunned and horrified by his reaction. It had never occurred to me that shyness could be mistaken for arrogance. While shyness and arrogance are worlds apart, they can appear quite similar. People generally do not give others the benefit of the doubt in this regard. Don't be mistaken as haughty or pretentious by keeping silent; it can cost you dearly. Start a casual conversation and let people experience your kindness. You know how much you appreciate the efforts others put forth in doing so. Make the same efforts yourself. Contrary to what your elders may have told you, silence is *not* golden when it comes to moving ahead in life.

Good Things Come *Only* to Those Who *Go Get* Them!

Waiting for someone to engage you in conversation will only result in a lot of lost time. Take the initiative. Don't spend another minute thinking that if you just keep waiting, interesting people will introduce themselves. It's just not going to happen, which I know all too well from personal experience. Usually, we are really waiting for someone we know—a friend, an associate or colleague, a client, even a competitor. We are comfortable with these people because we know them, have the same interests, know the same jargon, and are trying to meet people just like they are. We may end up paying a good amount to attend an event, and then waste it by just seeking out people we already know. Why? Because it's comfortable. Yet the purpose of the event was to make *new* contacts.

If ever there was a venue where you'd expect people to mix and mingle, it's a singles event. Yet they are notorious for attracting more shy people than a convention of periodontists! (I know this because my husband is a periodontist.) Most people at singles' events—including myself in my former life—spend most of their time uncomfortably waiting around, scanning the crowd for a friend. When a friend appears, he or she immediately begins spending the rest of the evening with that familiar person. If they wanted to be with one another, why didn't they just go out on a date or otherwise plan an evening out together? And if they don't want to do either, what are they doing spending time together? They're talking! Yes, talking—it's easy, comfortable, and safe. It is, however, no way to meet new people.

Good things come *only* to those who take the actions necessary to create them. American movie star and folk legend Will Rogers said, "Go out on a limb. That's where all the fruit is." He's right. Although it might be scary to venture beyond the safety of the trunk, you won't get any sweet fruit waiting there.

Be a Hero—*Take Responsibility for Meeting a New Person and Starting a Conversation with Him or Her*

Do you know what the biggest social fear is in America? Public speaking. The second? Meeting new people and starting conversations with them. So remember when you walk into a luncheon, a party, or some other event, many people may be scared to death to approach *you*. Fear of rejection actually keeps them from taking the meeting and talking plunge; but, in reality, the probability of rejection is quite small.

There are much riskier things in life than taking a chance on starting a conversation with someone you don't know. Furthermore, in the unlikely event your efforts are unappreciated, remember that it's doubtful you'll ever see that person again. But when your efforts are appreciated, you will be the hero by having started the conversation. You will gain stature, respect, and rapport by getting the conversation going. People will usually embrace your efforts and appreciate your leadership. After all, they probably wanted to make a new contact too, but may have been afraid to do so. You saved the day!

If your habit was to wait for someone else to take the initiative in starting a conversation, you may have been self-centered. You allowed your own comfort to take precedence over everyone else's. You weren't oing your fair share of the work. If you've largely ignored your conversational responsibilities, it's time to take charge. You cannot rely on the other person to carry the conversation for you—it's not supposed to be a monologue. And one-word answers to questions don't count as shouldering your share of the load.

To become a great conversationalist, it is essential to be invested in a conversation and actively work to help the other person feel comfortable. Take a look at the list of icebreaker questions that follow and make a commitment to use one the next time you meet a new person. If you are afraid you won't remember them, write them down, put the list in your pocket or purse, and refer to it before you go into the event. If you go blank, excuse yourself for a moment and walk into the restroom to take another look at the list.

The most famous and worn-out icebreaker is that age-old question, "What do you do for a living?" It's so standard that it didn't make the icebreaker list. Here are some other ways to begin a conversation that will provide a refreshing diversion from shoptalk. Be prepared to reciprocate, since your conversational partner is likely to return whatever questions you pose.

Fifty Ideas for Icebreakers

1. What is a typical day like for you?
2. If you could move anywhere in the world tomorrow, where would you go? Why?
3. What was the best job you ever had? What was the worst?
4. Tell me about the best vacation you've ever taken.

5. What's your favorite thing to do on a rainy day?
6. If you could replay any moment in your life, what would it be?
7. What one thing would you really like to own? Why?
8. Tell me about one of your favorite relatives.
9. What was it like in the town where you grew up?
10. What is your biggest dream or goal? Why?
11. What do you think is the perfect age? Why?
12. Of all the places you have ever lived, tell me about the one you liked the best.
13. What's your favorite holiday? What do you enjoy about it?
14. What family traditions do you particularly enjoy?
15. Tell me about the first car you ever bought.
16. Who were your heroes as a kid? Have they changed?
17. Describe a memorable teacher you had. Why was he or she so memorable?
18. Tell me about a movie or book that you've seen or read more than once.
19. What's your favorite restaurant? Why?
20. Tell me why you were named_____. What is the origin of your last name?
21. What you would do if you had all the time and money in the world?
22. What's the best surprise you've ever received?
23. What's the most fun surprise you've ever planned and pulled off for someone else?
24. Skiing here is always a great challenge. What are some of your favorite places to ski?
25. Who would star as you in a movie about your life? Why that person?
26. Who is the most famous person you've ever met?
27. What's the most unusual thing you've ever done?
28. Describe a costume that you wore to a party.
29. Are you alone by choice or by chance? How so?
30. Tell me about your dream house.
31. What song reminds you of an event in your life?

32. What's the most memorable meal you've eaten?
33. What's the most memorable coincidence you've experienced or heard about?
34. How are you able to tell if that melon is ripe?
35. What motion picture star would you like to interview? Why?
36. Tell me about your family.
37. What aroma brings forth a special memory?
38. Describe the kindest person you ever met.
39. What's your favorite thing to do alone?
40. Tell me about a childhood friend who used to get you in trouble.
41. Tell me about what you'd love to do for a living.
42. Describe your first away-from-home living quarters or experience.
43. What's your fantasy of a romantic evening out with your spouse?
44. Tell me about a time that you lost a job.
45. Share a memory of one of your grandparents.
46. Describe an embarrassing moment you've had.
47. Tell me something most people would never guess about you.
48. What would you do if you won one million dollars?
49. What's the most challenging part of your job?
50. How has the Internet affected your life?

"When some-one gives us a smile, our natural inclination is to smile back—even to someone we've never met. So use your smile as a tool to meet new people."

— Debra Fine

-3-

Take the Plunge—
Meet a New Person and
Start a Conversation!

"You no longer need to be concerned about avoiding people because you've forgotten their names. Assume the responsibility by asking for their names, and chances are you'll go on to have very pleasant conversations."
—Debra Fine—

You are armed with a pocket or purse full of icebreakers. You can greet anyone because you've got some great material. Just having topics to talk about is a great start and goes a long way toward helping you improve your people-meeting skills. However, there are still a few gaps that can create needless concern.

Right now you may feel prepared to respond only when someone else engages you in conversation. So you might walk into your son's school and wait for another parent to say hello. You may go to an industry dinner and try to act busy while you hope for a colleague to come along and talk. No. No. No. It does not need to be so stressful.

You *can* start the conversation—yes, *you!* It's easier than you may think. The best part is that it puts you more in charge of your own destiny. Instead of waiting for someone—*anyone*—to talk to you, *you* choose your conversational partner. What a concept: You get to select someone instead of standing around feeling rejected. Why you may even enjoy it!

The rules are simple. Just think about it. When someone gives us a smile, our natural inclination is to smile back. So lead the way. Be the first to smile and say hi to someone you've ever met. That's pretty easy. Just a smile, a friendly hello, and you're in—almost. In addition to that, also be sure to make eye contact. These simple acts are the beginnings of rapport. In those few seconds, you have taken an interest in another person.

Now, if the thought of doing this makes you want to jump into bed and pull the covers over your head, start flashing your pearly whites in a setting that requires nothing more than that. For example, walk through a mall and just say hello to ten people as you pass them by. When you walk through the parking lot to go into the grocery store, be sure to greet three other shoppers. Keep doing this until it feels natural and becomes a habit.

What's in a Name?

Okay, now it's time to actually stay and talk—not just offer a passing hello. Make it a point to remember the other person's name. Learning and using names is probably the single most important rule of good conversation, so stay focused during the introduction. Repeat the name back in your greeting, "Nice to meet you, Debra." To help yourself commit the name to memory, immediately use the person's name in the conversation. Refrain from thinking about your reply and concentrate on the other person's name. Focus on the name, repeat it, and then formulate your answer.

If you do get distracted during the introduction and miss the name, confess! Don't go through the whole conversation pretending you know the person's name. It's better to say something like, "Excuse me, I didn't get your name." It is always preferable to have the other party repeat it than for you to fake it. Never ever fake knowing someone's name! This is especially true when you run into someone you've previously met whose name you cannot recall. Don't wait for Divine intervention! Say, "I'm so sorry. I've forgotten your name. Please remind me."

You no longer need to be concerned about avoiding someone simply because you've forgotten his or her name. Assume the responsibility, by asking once again, what the person's name is, and chances are you'll go on to have a very pleasant conversation. Even if you're on the other side of a crowded room or passing in the grocery store, go over and greet that person. If you avoid someone because you are embarrassed over having forgotten his or her name, you've just compounded the error with rudeness.

Individuals with foreign or unusual names get slighted more than the rest of us. Make it a point to learn the proper pronunciation, even if it means asking the other person to repeat it a few times, and maybe even write it down. When you take the time to learn another person's name, you are expressing a sincere interest in that individual that will be warmly received. Conversely, if you get lazy and don't—because someone has a difficult name—you are sending a message that he or she isn't worth your time.

It is always worth the effort to remember names. In fact, learning names is part of hosting the conversation. A host is always expected to know and use everyone's name, since he is responsible for making introductions as new people enter the conversation. I was seated at a table for eight and met three people who arrived at the table before I did. As others came, I extended my hand, introduced myself and made the introductions to the other three. I said, "This is Linda with

Sun Microsystems, and Jon with Lucent Technologies, and Sam from the Association of Safety Engineers." Acting as the host puts everyone at ease, and creates an atmosphere of warmth and appreciation that naturally encourages conversation. The other people will appreciate your leadership because you helped put them at ease.

Nix Nicknames—*Ask People What They Like to Be Called*

If someone introduces himself as "Michael," don't call him "Mike." If he wanted you to call him "Mike," he would have said so. If someone has a difficult name, make the effort to learn it—do not shorten it to a nickname without permission!

Make sure you use people's names and, again, get them right! For instance, I call a client whose secretary answers, "Katherine Winter's office, this is Susan." I respond by saying, "Hi Susan. This is Debra Fine. May I speak with Katherine?" Notice that I used each person's name and I did not take any liberties with them. Susan is very important because she represents the gateway to my client. It would not serve me to annoy her by slashing her name to "Sue," nor would it be helpful to avoid using her name all together. Using people's names shows you are interested in them. Using the names they desire shows you care.

Here's another example: I was at the video store one time returning a couple of overdue movies. I started talking to the clerk while we were waiting for the computer to process the late fees. In the course of our brief conversation I used his name and asked if he had seen every movie in the store. By the time my late fees showed up on-screen, he cancelled them and told me to have a nice day! When you use another person's name sincerely in a conversation, it helps that person feel special and, as a result, they'll be more inclined to treat you better.

Remember—*It's Better to Give than to Receive*

It's just as important to give *your* name when you meet someone—even if you've met that person before and think he or she should have remembered your name. Consider it a random act of kindness. For example, I would extend my hand and say, "Hi Patrick. Debra Fine. How are you?" By stating my name, I got Patrick off the hook. If he had forgotten my name, he was spared from embarrassment. He also didn't have to waste our conversational time by being distracted trying to recall my name.

As I mentioned, my husband is a periodontist. As a group, periodontists are not known for their charm or gregarious personalities. Frequently, when we go out, his patients recognize him and start conversations without reintroducing themselves. If my husband doesn't have a clue who they are, he feels awkward. He can't include me in the conversation easily because he can't get through the introductions.

Don't assume that someone who sees you infrequently will remember your name—especially when you are seen out of context. For example, you will remember the realtor who spent a Sunday driving you around looking at houses easier than he or she is likely to remember you—especially if you are in a sweatsuit at the gas station. Give the realtor a break; offer your name when you say hello, and recall the time when you were together.

"Icebreakers are not only good ways to start conversations, but they can also be statements with accompanying questions you can use to keep the conversation going. Be direct so there is absolutely no doubt you are starting a dialogue rather than just being polite."

—Debra Fine

-4-

Keep the Conversation Going!

*"Showing genuine interest in someone else is
complimentary, and it's essential to conversing."*
—Debra Fine—

Again, remember, instead of sitting back and waiting for some kind soul to walk up to you and start a conversation, take the lead. Think of it as though you've invited that person to your home for dinner. As host, it's your job to see that your guest is comfortable. The same is true when meeting a new person—do your best to make your "guest" as comfortable as possible.

When you walk into a party, a gathering, or anywhere you go, make it a priority to meet some new people. And since it's much easier to engage in conversation with one rather than a group, begin by looking for an "approachable person." You could also engage an "approachable couple," but for ease of discussion, we'll just use "approachable person." Once you become more adept at casual conversation, virtually everyone becomes approachable.

The approachable person gives you eye contact, or at least is not already engaged in conversation. It's the person getting something to eat, standing near you in line, sitting alone at a table or in a waiting room, or the one crossing the room alone. More often than not, they are pleased when someone initiates a conversation. Believe me, I've been around plenty of these folks. They are intelligent, interesting, welcoming, and shy (even if they appear aloof)—but certainly not to be feared. Remember, they are in the same spot you were in before you decided to improve your people-meeting and conversational skills. As you reach out more to others, you'll expand your horizons and enrich your life.

Make it a point to look around a room or location when you first enter it. It doesn't matter what the event is—a meeting, reception, baby shower, party, car show, family reunion, or wherever people gather. You'll see people standing, walking, or perhaps sitting alone. Don't wait. Make eye contact and be the first to smile. You'll probably get a smile back and put the other person at ease—just like a fine host! People are then more likely to reward you by being attentive listeners, giving you opportunities to practice your icebreakers.

Icebreakers are not only good ways to start conversations, but they can also be statements with accompanying questions you can use to *keep the conversation going.* However, don't just use statements that don't request specific information. Doing so is like lobbing the conversational ball blindfolded, not having any idea where it will land or whether it even has the chance of getting tossed back. For example, enthusiastic exclamations like "What a beautiful day" or "That was a great ____" are indirect and therefore not strong invitations to chat. Be direct so there is absolutely no doubt you are starting a dialogue rather than just being polite. For example, make these statements and ask these questions:

Questions to Start and Keep Conversations Going

- What a beautiful day. What is your favorite thing about spring?

- I was truly touched by that movie. How did you like it? Why?
- This is a wonderful restaurant. What is your favorite restaurant? Why?
- What a great conference! Can you tell me about the sessions you attended?
- I was absent last week. Would you describe what happened?
- That was an interesting program after lunch. What did you think?
- Presidential campaigns seem to start immediately after the inauguration. What do you think of the campaign process?
- Pursuing a dream or goal sure makes life an adventure. What are some of your dreams and goals?
- I am excited about our new mayor. How and why do you think her administration will be different from her predecessors'?
- Your lawn always looks so green. What is your secret?
- We've been working together for months now. I'd like to get to know you better. Would you tell me about some of your outside interests?
- You worked pretty hard on that stair stepper. What other equipment do you use?
- You always wear such attractive clothes. What are your favorite places to shop?
- We have one daughter and she keeps us busy. How do you manage to run a house with four children?
- I read in the newspaper that our governor has taken another trip overseas. What do you think of all his travel?

Parties of Five or More

It can be more of a challenge, especially for a people-meeting/conversational novice, to break into a group of five or more. Larger groups are usually well entrenched, and it requires more strategic action to be welcomed by them. Use these approaches when you find it necessary or desirable to get engaged with these folks:

- Show an interest in the speaker, but stand slightly away from the group. A group this size may be slow to warm so first let them become accustomed to seeing you. It may not be immediate, but as long as you are pleasant and show interest in them, it's likely they will bring you into their circle.
- Ease into the group by demonstrating that you've been listening. Look for welcoming signs such as someone asking your opinion or physically shifting position to better include you.
- Initially, it is best to find a point of agreement; barring that, just acknowledge the speaker. Wait before rocking the boat with a big wave of differing opinions. Before offering your views, let the group warm to you. If you come on too strong too fast, the group will resent your intrusion and disband. Then you'll need to start all over again, looking for someone to chat with whom you haven't just offended!

Extend the Hand of Friendship—*Take an Interest in Others*

It's the effort that counts—as imperfect as it may seem. What matters is taking the plunge and starting the conversation. Show an interest in what the other person says. Showing genuine interest is complimentary, and it's essential to conversing. When you are interested in how I lost 65 pounds, how I started my business, or anything else about me, I feel special. I also think positively about you and want to continue talking with you. The more interest you show in me, the more interesting you become to me. The simple act of truly being interested in the other person has an amazing effect on a conversation—it just snowballs.

You will be successful at meeting new people and starting conversations when you take the initiative and just go do it. You'll be surprised by how easy it is and at the positive reinforcement you get from others when you start a conversation. Remember to use the following five steps and you are well on your way to an excellent chat:

1. Smile.
2. Make eye contact.
3. Find the approachable person.
4. Offer your name and use the other person's name several times.
5. Throw out an icebreaker.

Do these things as soon as possible. You'll discover how worthwhile they really are. The true effort is in taking the risk to be the first to say hello. There is no perfect icebreaker— just do your best to launch the interaction. It's then up to the other person to allow you to engage in a conversation or not. Think about it. We all do that. We size someone up, determine if we are in the mood to chat, and gauge whether it is worth the investment of time to chat with the approaching person. The person being approached may have already decided on his or her willingness to respond—regardless of the words said.

Appreciate Differences—*and Look for Common Ground*

People often make the mistake of assuming they have nothing in common with others. We may easily allow differences of all kinds to bias us against engaging in conversations. We might allow things like gender, ethnicity, social status, generation, occupation, or a host of other differences to create artificial barriers to conversational success.

In the course of touring the U.S. and talking to thousands of people in every geographic region, from all walks of life, I have discovered that we are all more alike than we are different. It's simply a matter of talking, showing an interest, and listening. When I approach someone and engage in a conversation, it's like I'm slowly peeling an onion—one layer at a time. I am always amazed and gratified by how interesting and worthwhile it is to take the time to talk with someone I don't yet know.

At one of the first programs I ever presented, I asked everyone to introduce him- or herself and share why coming to a session on casual conversation was of interest. The first person to introduce himself was a gentleman named Bob. He said he was attending because he was a customer service engineer and his boss wanted him to improve his conversational skills with customers. He added that although his boss sent him to the session, he was glad because he'd just moved to the very small town of Elizabeth, Colorado. As a single man alone, he felt isolated and wanted to meet some new people. Here's what followed:

"Hi! My name is Bob, and I'm from Elizabeth, Colorado."

"I, too, used to live in Elizabeth, next to the Douglas county line near the town of Parker. Are you there or closer to the town of Elizabeth itself?"

"No, I now live near Parker, as well, in a development called Ponderosa Park Estates."

"Ponderosa Park Estates? Wow. Bob, I used to live there too! I lived right near Ponderosa Lane and Overlook Road."

"Well, Debra, I live on Overlook Road."

"That is amazing, Bob. I lived in the log house at 120 Overlook Road."

"Well, Debra, this is truly amazing because I live in the log house at 120 Overlook Road!"

It turns out that the family to whom we sold the home in 1985 had moved, and sold it to Bob in 1991. Because of this chance encounter, and because I took an interest in the fact that Bob was from Elizabeth, Bob invited me to bring my family over to see the house again. I was delighted. We went there and the kids got to experience part of their own history they could not recall because they were so young when we lived there.

Keep making the effort to reach out and take an interest in people, and you'll be richly rewarded. You have two jumbo-sized lists of icebreakers to help you get started. You can create lots more as you go along.

"Whenever you begin a dialogue with a question, be ready to dig deeper so that the other person knows you are interested in hearing more. With the appropriate queries, a conversation with a coworker or prospect about the weekend can easily occupy the time it takes to drink an entire cup of coffee."

—Debra Fine

-5-

Let's Give Them Something to Talk About

"When you are an astute observer, you'll notice that your new acquaintance is giving you a wealth of free information you can use to keep a conversation going."
—Debra Fine—

Y ou've smiled, made eye contact, found the approachable person, offered your name, and repeated his or hers. What's left, you ask? Plenty! Have no fear—this is where it really gets to be fun. If you are introverted, you will love this part because you stay on the quiet side. Your mission is to get your conversation partner talking about him or herself. Most people enjoy the opportunity to share their stories, and if you give them the chance, they'll start talking. This is a no-brainer route to conversational success.

It's All in the Asking

By asking open-ended questions, you offer your conversational partner the opportunity to disclose as much or as little as that person wants. These questions call for more than a simple yes or no answer, yet they make no stressful demands.

Your conversational partner will decide how much he or she feels comfortable saying. Such questions are especially effective with one-word-answer co-workers, kids, neighbors, in-laws, industry colleagues, prospects, friends, associates, and when first meeting someone. The key to successfully using open-ended questions is choosing the right question and then following up with another, if it's needed.

For instance, let's take the toughest conversational partners of all—school-aged kids. They may make it so difficult to have a conversation that it might almost be an oxymoron to consider kids as conversational partners. Nevertheless, because they are kids, I give them the benefit of the doubt and hone my skills with my own two kids. I know I haven't lost my edge when I can get them engaged in meaningful dialogue!

For example, my kids come through the door at the end of the day and I ask, "How was your day at school?" In stereo, I get back, "Fine." Instead of considering that a dead-end, I follow up with another question: "What did you like about it today?" My 16-year-old son usually says, "I don't know." I look him right in the eye and tell him, "Really, tell me about one class you liked today." He thinks about it for a minute. Finally he says, "Science." And I inquire, "What did you like about science?" He launches into a colorful description of an experiment they did, and all of a sudden we're talking. The bottom line is that you need to open up the lines of communication by showing you truly care.

Digging Deeper

Every Monday, in workplaces everywhere, people ask each other, "How was your weekend?" That question most often results in a one-sentence reply akin to, "Good. How about yours?" Before a reply is uttered, you may be ten steps past him or her. What's the message? You really weren't interested; you were just saying hello. "How was your vacation?" "How was your holiday?" "How's work?" "How are you?" "What's been going on?" "How have you been?" are only a few other ways to say hello. It's almost universally understood that these questions are a form of greeting, not sincere inquiries. They are not really open-ended questions.

Most of the time the conversation ends immediately after a brief exchange. I ask my husband Steve, "How was your day?" He replies, "Great." The conversation evaporates not because there was no place to go with it, but because of a lack of follow-through. My husband doesn't think I really care about his day unless I ask more. I invite his conversation by asking, "Why was it great? What went on for you today?"

Whenever you begin a dialogue with a question, be ready to dig deeper so that the other person knows you are interested in hearing more. Here are some ways to do so:

- "How was your summer?" "Excellent." "What special things did you do?"
- "How were your holidays?" "Pretty good." "What kinds of things did you do?"
- "How was your weekend?" "Good." "What did you do?" "I went to see that new play down at the Civic Center." "Really? You're interested in _____? I never knew that. Tell me more about that."
- "How was your vacation?" "Great" "What did you enjoy most about it?" "We went deep-sea fishing...."
- "What do you usually do for fun?" "Boat or fish—sometimes swim." "What attracted you to boating?"

With the appropriate queries, a conversation with a co-worker or prospect about the weekend can easily occupy the time it takes to drink an entire cup of coffee. The key is to take a genuine interest in what the other person is saying, along with a genuine desire to hear the response to your questions. So, while you get to be quiet, you do not get to be passive. You need to actively participate in the conversation.

Suppose, however, you call a customer or your boss and the conversation goes as follows when you ask about the weekend:

"How was your weekend?" "Great." "Tell me about it." "Well, we spent some time working in the garden and that was about it. Now, how about this proposal?"

You need to recognize that the other person has steered the conversation back to business. That's the signal that the person does not want to chat at the moment. Respect those wishes by switching back to a business mode.

Here are some other examples of digging deeper into a conversation. You ask, "How have you been?" and get the reply, "Busy." Your responses could include: "How do you deal with being busy?" "What is going on that's got you so busy?" "Describe a busy day for you." "Do you like being busy?" "Does there seem to be a cycle of busyness during your year?" "Do you remember a time in your life that you weren't as busy?"

Or you may ask, "Isn't this weather beautiful?" and receive the reply, "It sure is." You might respond with these questions: "How warm does it get in this part of the country?" "What is your idea of an ideal climate?" "How does lovely weather affect you? What are you inclined to do?" "Have you lived anywhere else with weather as temperate as this?" "What brought you here?"

Of course, it may be easier to ask appropriate open-ended questions of people you know than people you are just meeting. Use discretion when meeting new people. Asking a difficult question could put the other person in an awkward position. Likewise, sometimes when we are asking open-ended questions, we really are asking questions that require only a word or two to answer. Here are a few new ways to ask some old favorites:

Instead of asking this:	Ask this:
Are you married?	Would you tell me about your family?
What do you do for a living?	Would you tell me about your business/work?
Do you have kids?	Would you tell me about your family?
What's your favorite hobby?	Would you tell me about your favorite hobby?
How was your weekend?	Would you tell me about the best part of your weekend?

When you need to mingle at an industry function or are to have lunch with a client or prospect, prepare yourself for the event by selecting some business-related questions to ask. Here are some that work every time. Of course, the goal is not to ask every one of these, but to have some ready so that you feel prepared, which will enable you to be calm and confident.

Failsafe Questions for Every Business Function

- How did you get started in your business?
- How did you come up with this idea?
- What got you interested in_____(business function, job, industry)?
- What happened first?
- Tell me what you enjoy most about your profession.

- What separates your company from the competition?
- Describe some of the challenges of your profession.
- What will be the coming trends in your business?
- What ways have you found to be the most effective in promoting your business?
- Tell me about your most important work experience.
- What advice would you give someone just starting out in your business?
- What one thing would you do if you knew for sure that you couldn't fail?
- What significant changes have you seen since you started in your field?
- What is the most unusual incident that you've ever experienced in your business?
- How has the Internet impacted your business? What about your profession as a whole?
- What would you do if time and money were no object?

Free for the Taking

Astute observers discover that their new conversational partners give them a wealth of free information, which they can use to keep conversations going.

For example, inviting someone to tell you about his or her family or job by asking open-ended questions, brings you additional information that you can use to further the conversation. Suppose you asked me, "Debra, how is it that you worked in product planning for AT&T?" and I'd say, "I was in R&D (Research and Development) in Buffalo, New York, where I'm from, and I hated it. I hated being an engineer—they don't even make pocket protectors for women! So, I asked to be transferred anywhere. They brought me to Denver to work in product planning." I offered lots of free information: I'm from Buffalo; I was in R&D; and I hated being an engineer. You can choose any of that free information to find more about me that interests you the most. You could have facilitated our conversation by asking me any one of a number of open-ended questions, including but not limited to:

- How bad are the winters in Buffalo? Is it as snowy as they say?
- Why didn't you like being an engineer?
- What difference would it have made in your career if there had been pocket protectors for women?
- What is it like to do R&D for a corporation like AT&T?

Conversational Catalysts

Lapel pins and jewelry: The man behind me in line at the bakery was wearing a lapel pin on his suit. I asked him about it and found out that he's in the local Rotary Club. I shared with him that I was a Rotarian as well. From that simple beginning, we had a great conversation.

Team apparel and other logo-identified clothing, accessories, water bottles, and clipboards are great conversation catalysts. Some ideas: "It looks like you might be a fan of the _____. What do you think of their season?" or "I notice that you're wearing a shirt from the _____. Have you ever been there? What did you think of it?" or "I see that you ran the 'Race for the Cure.' What other races have you run?"

Office and home decorations provide catalysts for conversations to occur. A diploma on the wall gives you an opening. For example, "Why did you choose to do your graduate work at the University of Michigan?" Virtually any object or photograph on display is a conversation starter, for instance. "You must love golf—tell me about this trophy;" or "What an interesting piece of art. Tell me about it;" or "Tell me about this picture. Who is that with you?"

Location, location, location, and occasion, occasion, occasion. Both the occasion and location of an event offer a wide variety of free information. Here are some great questions to ask: At a wedding: "I was the bride's college roommate. How do you know the couple?" At a meeting or other large gathering: "What brought you to this event?" is an easy and unobtrusive way to start a conversation.

I was leaving a seminar I just gave, holding the elevator for a man coming down the hall. I usually don't meet people and start conversations on elevators because of the limited time available to chat, but on a whim used the free information I had—I knew there were two classrooms on that floor. Since the man hadn't been in my class, there was a pretty good chance that he'd come from the other one. I asked, "Were you here for a class?" He said he had been in a book-writing class.

It turns out that I was speaking with Harry MacLean, best-selling author and teacher of the course. We continued our conversation outside the elevator, and I now have a new friend. He even agreed to speak to my book club about his most recent book, *Once Upon a Time*. One of the reasons I love casual conversation is that you just never know who you'll meet or where it'll lead.

When you are observant, you'll get a lot of free information from people's behavior. The way others speak and write can give you the opportunity to meet them. Notice if they are left-handed. You can ask, "Is it challenging being left-handed? What pet peeves do you have about it?" Does the person have an accent? If so, you might say, "I thought I heard an accent. What part of the country/world are you from?" or "What brought you here?" or "What do you miss most about where you are from?" or "What do you enjoy most about living here?"

I entered my local FedEx office with efficiency in mind—after all, that's why I was there—I wanted to get in and get out. The fact that I needed FedEx service is free information that I'm in a hurry. I've got a pressing delivery. However, as I watched the clerk complete the forms, I was struck by the beautiful handwriting this left-handed woman had. I complimented her with a statement—not a question. Unfortunately, she responded as though it were an inquiry. I got the whole story of how she used to be a teacher and had purposefully perfected her handwriting...she moved to Arizona...got divorced...remarried and moved to Colorado. I could not get her to understand that I was in a hurry. She was still talking as I backed out of the door!

Just Start with a Smile—*and Take an Interest in Others*

Now that you are becoming more familiar with meeting new people and engaging them in conversation, keep doing the fundamentals. Can you recall five sure-fire questions to use in a business setting? Can you name a half-dozen sources of free information? Observe your current location right now. What do you see that would make good conversational material?

You'll get better at all of this the same way you've improved at other activities, simply by doing it. It's not difficult—high school geometry was probably much harder than this. Just start with a smile and take an interest in others. Little by little, you'll give each of your new-found conversational partners plenty to talk about.

"When the three elements of attentive listening—visual, verbal, and mental—are combined, powerful listening results. The talker will love it and be more inclined to like you."

—Debra Fine

-6-

Generously Give the Gift of Listening

"Don't jeopardize a relationship by failing to listen when the other person is speaking."
—Debra Fine—

We've covered half of the ingredients used in meeting new people—how to take the lead, break the ice, and maintain a conversation. You now know what works and what doesn't. However, none of this guarantees any success.

Once it begins, a great conversation hinges on two things—talking *and* listening. Scientific research has shown that people can listen at the rate of approximately 300 words a minute. On the flip side, most of us can speak at only 150-200 words a minute—unless you're one of those folks rattling off all the exclusions at the end of a radio ad to lease a new car!

The dilemma is that we have the capacity to take in much more information than one person can possibly divulge at any given time. So what do we do with this excess capacity? Why, of course, we put it to use. We eavesdrop on other conversations; we start thinking about what to have for dinner;

we drift away into our private thoughts and suddenly we've drifted too far—and missed something important.

Ten Tips for Tip-Top Listening

1. Learn to *want* to listen to others. The desire, interest, concentration, and self-discipline necessary will grow out of caring about them.
2. To let the other person know you are a good listener, give verbal and visual cues that you are listening.
3. Anticipate excellence. We get good information more often when we expect it.
4. Become a "whole body" listener. Listen with your ears, your eyes, and your heart.
5. Take notes. They aid retention.
6. Listen now; report later. Plan to tell someone what you heard and you will remember it better.
7. Build rapport by being sensitive to the other person. Approximate his or her gestures, facial expressions, and voice patterns to create a comfortable atmosphere.
8. Control internal and external distractions.
9. Generously give the gift of listening.
10. Be present; eliminate any tendency to daydream. Don't drift off and lose focus on your conversational partner.

Psychologist Carl Rogers said, "The biggest block to personal conversation is one man's inability to listen intelligently, understandingly, and skillfully to another person." Psychoanalyst Dr. Ann Appelbaum understood the source of her livelihood when she wrote in The Menninger Clinic's newsletter, *Perspective,* "The image of the voice crying in the wilderness epitomizes the loneliness, the madness of not being heard. So great is our need and hunger for validation that good listeners are prized. Psychoanalysts, for example, earn a living by listening and providing responses that validate the other person."

Have you ever gone out to lunch with someone who really needed to talk? You hardly said a word. You offered support, a few kind words, nodded your head, and listened. The other person felt much better afterwards and is still ever so grateful for the "conversation." So few people take the time to listen that you'll stand out as an extraordinarily caring person.

Listening Is *Seen—Not Just Heard*

In our technology-driven world, we are so bombarded by distracting stimuli and demands on our time that it's a challenge to listen. Listening is no longer taken for granted. In fact, it's frequently the exception. But when the three elements of attentive listening—visual, verbal, and mental—are combined, powerful listening results. The talker will love it and be more inclined to like you.

The physiological process of listening is invisible to the observer. We cannot watch sound vibrations as they go into someone's ears to confirm that the intended message has been received. Consequently, the person speaking needs to be on the lookout for visual cues to validate receipt of the message. Visual cues from you are the best indicators you can use to let your conversational partner know you are paying attention. Facial expressions, head nods, hand gestures, and positive body language are clear ways of expressing interest in the other person and what he or she is saying.

Eight-year-old Nicholas came home from school, bounded into the house, and started telling his dad about the terrific day he just had. "Dad," Nick said, "I had a great day at school. We had art class today and I painted a cool picture of the mountains. We played soccer during gym and I scored a goal. And guess what? They served pizza for lunch!"

Nicholas sees his dad reading the newspaper and sighs, "Dad, you're not listening to me." His dad looks up and says, "Yes, I am, son. You painted a picture of the mountains, you scored a goal in the soccer game, and you had pizza for lunch." Nicholas, unappeased, replies, "No, Dad. That's not it. You're not listening to me with your eyes."

Even though Nick's dad clearly heard his son, Nick felt minimized because he did not have his dad's full attention. He wanted more than a download of facts about his day from his dad. He wanted to *see* his dad's response. He wanted to *feel* connected. He wanted his dad to be *invested* in the story. He wanted validation *while* he was telling his story.

Listening is more than just hearing words. It's a level of involvement that goes beyond merely reciting the contents of a conversation. Ray Birdwhistle, a pioneer in nonverbal communication, estimated that in a normal two-person conversation, verbal components carry less than 35 percent of the social meaning of the situation, while nonverbal components account for over 65 percent. It's critical to maintain eye contact when you are listening to another person. Don't be discourteous by looking around at what others are doing—stay focused on the person with whom you are conversing.

Again, body language gives the other person clues about you and your listening. When you cross your arms and legs, you are exhibiting defensiveness—even if your reason is a cold temperature. If you keep your head down and avoid eye contact, you send a message that you are avoiding interaction—even if your reason is shyness and you actually want someone to talk to you! People generally respond to those signals by ignoring you; you are not considered approachable. If you rest your chin in your hand, it appears that you are bored. Likewise, when you place your hands on your hips, you appear aggressive and unhappy with your conversational partner, or with the words you are hearing.

There are just as many ways to signal your interest and enthusiasm for the dialogue. You give positive messages to the person talking when you:

- Lean forward.
- Maintain eye contact.
- Open up your arms.
- Relax your body posture.
- Face your partner.
- Nod and smile.

Unlike other conversational skills that may be easier for you, it requires practice and concentration to overcome nervous habits and use positive body language. Stick with it though, and it will eventually become second nature to you.

You can also increase the comfort level of your conversational partner by modifying your own style to be more similar to the other person's. If you are chatting with someone who speaks slowly and softly, keep your volume down also. You can overwhelm a slow-talking, soft-spoken person with your own volume and speed. This is not to say you shouldn't be yourself; you need to be. However, as the "host," you need to do whatever you can to enhance the comfort of your "guest."

Verbalize Your Listening

Verbal cues complement the visual cues you give a speaker. The absence of verbal cues makes the person speaking wonder if anyone is listening. I called my dad, who lives in Buffalo. I was telling him a story about the kids and there was silence on the other end of the phone. I abruptly stopped the story and asked, "Dad, are you *there*?" He became indignant and said, "Of course I'm here. I'm listening to you. Tell me about my grandkids." I replied, "You weren't saying anything so I thought maybe you had suddenly been buried by eight feet of snow." "I just didn't want to interrupt," he replied.

There are numerous verbal cues to let the talker know you are fully engaged in the conversation. These brief comments tell the talker you are interested and want to know more. You can use verbal cues to show you have a positive response, disagree, want to hear more about something in particular, or something else. Check out this list to see which cues are used in different situations:

If you want to show that you are:	Say:
Wanting More About an Idea	Tell me more. What was that like for you?
Taking It All In	Hmmm, I see….
Responding Positively	How interesting! What an accomplishment!
Diverging	On the other hand, what do you think…?
Expanding on the Idea	Along that same line, do you…? Why?
Arguing/Refuting	What proof do you have of that?
Involving Yourself	Could I do that? What would it mean to me?
Clarifying	I'm not sure I'm clear on your feelings about….

Empathizing	That must have been tough/frustrating, etc.
General to Specific	Can you give me an example?
Specific to General	What's the big picture here?
Present to Future	What do you think will happen next?
Present to Past	What happened first?
Likeness/Difference	Have you ever seen anything like this? What's the opposing point of view?
Extremes/Contrasts	What's the downside? Or What's the optimum?

Other verbal listening cues function to redirect the conversation by transitioning to another topic. Examples of cues that offer a seamless segue include:

- That reminds me of....
- When you were talking about ____, I remembered....
- You know, I was just reading in the paper about....
- I've always wanted to ask you....
- I thought of you when I heard....
- Do you mind if I change the subject? There's something I've wanted to ask of someone with your expertise.

All of the above verbal cues indicate that you are fully present. Just as important, they encourage the other person to keep speaking. Imagine someone asks you a question and you respond with a one-sentence answer. You are uncertain as to how much information they are truly interested in learning. Added verbal cues, as you respond, give them confidence that your interest is sincere. Verbal cues let others know they may continue. Use verbal cues as an active way to get others to do the talking so you can spend some time eating your salad!

Quiet people often congratulate themselves for their awesome listening skills. They say, "Gabby people never listen; at least we quiet types keep our mouths shut and listen!" This attitude is reflected in the lack of participation in the conversation. It is important to verbally let others know we are following along, actively listening. Quiet people are invisible or, even worse, observers rather than contributors.

Stating the Obvious

When you paraphrase what's been said, or repeat the specifics of what you have heard, there can be no doubt that you have listened and understood the speaker. This is especially effective when you are disagreeing with your conversational partner or have listened to that person explain something highly complex or technical. Paraphrasing the speaker clarifies that you understood accurately. Or it can help the speaker recognize that you misunderstood what he or she was attempting to communicate. For instance, let's say I am unhappy with what I perceive as a lack of help from my husband in doing household chores. We discuss the problem and I am thrilled; Steve promises to help more around the house.

Two weeks later, I jump all over Steve. I am upset because I have not witnessed his added help around the house. "You promised to help more with household chores. When do you plan on keeping your promise?" I implore. "I *am* helping out," Steve replies. "I've been collecting the trash and taking it to the curb every Thursday." "That's it?" I ask. I expected Steve to take on 50 percent of the chores. But instead of clarifying what he meant by agreeing to my request for help, I assumed I knew what he meant. He assumed I meant *any* help would be appreciated. Men and women (and children) will say exactly the same words; yet can mean two entirely different things. Clarify or paraphrase to prevent misunderstandings at work, at home, and everywhere else.

In an emotionally charged situation, you gain a side benefit of defusing anger when you repeat the specifics of what the other person said. People naturally calm down when they realize they've been understood. For example, skilled customer service managers know that by repeating what an angry customer is saying, they can reduce the level of hostility; remaining calm while doing so sends a message about your own poise and professionalism.

Before expressing apologies or resolving a situation, let the person know that he or she has been heard by repeating the specifics.

Staying Focused on Your Conversational Partner

All the visual and verbal cues in the world are useless if you haven't stayed focused enough on the conversation to track it. A good conversational partner retains what's been said. If you are too bored to stay with the conversation, exit gracefully instead of embarrassing your conversational partner by demonstrating boredom.

I had a business lunch with a woman who shall remain nameless. I told her a story about my kids and mentioned that my husband is a periodontist. Several minutes later, during a pause in the conversation, she asked if I was married! Clearly, she had drifted away in the conversation.

Don't jeopardize a relationship by failing to listen. Your job as a conversational partner is to listen when the other person is speaking. This isn't optional—*it's a required courtesy when conversing*. If, for whatever reason, you cannot remain focused on what the speaker is saying, excuse yourself. The messages you send through visual, verbal, and mental cues let your partner know the status of the conversation. If you feel trapped in a conversation and don't know how to exit, read on. We'll take care of that dilemma as well.

"Don't jeopardize a relationship by failing to listen. Your job as a conversational partner is to listen when the other person is speaking. This isn't optional—it's a required courtesy when conversing."

—Debra Fine

"It's up to you to either invigorate the conversation or allow it to grind to a slow halt. Do your part to charge up the conversation. Be prepared with questions about the background and history of the people you're about to talk with."

—Debra Fine

-7-

Prevent Pregnant Pauses with Preparation

"Building trust and intimacy over time builds friendships."
—Debra Fine—

E ven with icebreakers, conversation makers, and active listening, there are still times when a conversation can grind to a halt if you're not prepared.

Invariably, at any conference luncheon, at least one table has eight intelligent people staring at their plates trying to figure out how to get the conversation rolling after they've "talked shop" ten minutes too long! They could have avoided extensive examination of the rice pilaf if just one person had been prepared. Yes, be prepared—as in doing advance planning.

All eight knew that they would be sitting down with seven other people they didn't know. A good conversationalist plans before the event. Don't worry—slides, laptop presentations, and laser pointers are not required! All that is needed is a bit of forethought that can be accomplished in the car on the way to the event.

Don't Let Old Acquaintances Be Forgotten
You need more than icebreakers to enjoy your time conversing with others. You need to tailor your preparation to

the nature of the occasion and the people with whom you'll be talking. One of the toughest conversational partners—after kids—is an acquaintance you see only once in a while. You have some history together, you know a bit about each other, but you don't have a clue about what's changed in the year since you last saw each other. In fact, it's good to assume that things have probably changed.

Suppose you see a colleague annually at an industry function. During the past twelve months, he or she may have taken a different job or started a business, experienced the death of a close friend or relative, gone on an extraordinary vacation, had a spiritual awakening, gotten married or divorced, or whatever. In other words, don't presume that you are picking up a conversation that was held a year ago. Find out what's new and keep the conversation rolling with questions like these:

- Bring me up to date on....
- What's been going on at work since I've seen you?
- What has changed in your life since we last spoke?
- How has your year been?
- What's new with the family?

Getting a History Lesson

At times, you'll find yourself in an awkward silence or a pregnant pause. It's up to you to either invigorate the conversation or allow it to grind to a slow halt. Do your part to charge up the conversation. Be prepared to ask questions about the background and history of the people you're about to talk with. For instance, you could ask:

- How did you two meet?
- How did you get started _____?
- What got you interested in this area?

- When did you first know you wanted to be a _____?
- What brought you to (location)?
- How do you all know each other?
- What got you interested in _____?
- What gave you the idea for this business?
- What happened first?

Prepare for the Long Haul—*Ask "Interview" Questions*

Prepare for a conversation like you'd prepare for an interview—both as the interviewer and the interviewee. It takes much less effort to prepare for a conversation than a job interview, but the philosophy is the same. Have material prepared that is relevant to the event so you can converse articulately and gracefully. I call the questions that fall into this category "Interview Questions"—they help keep the conversation humming along.

As I drive into a parking lot before entering a meeting, luncheon, or any other type of function, I plan as if I'm doing an interview. I spend two minutes thinking about specific interview questions that apply to the person(s), event, or situation I am about to encounter. Most of us find ourselves across from someone in silence, cannot think of anything to talk about, and panic. What an awkward moment! Think about it. When is the worst time to think of something to talk about? When there is nothing to talk about! Here are some examples of interview questions you can customize to fit your own personality:

- What do you enjoy most about this time of the year?
- What got you involved in this organization/event?
- If you weren't here, what would you be doing at this very moment?
- If you could meet any one person, who would it be?
- Tell me about an issue that matters a great deal to you.
- What has been your most important work experience?

- What word would you say best describes you?
- Do you have a personal motto or creed?
- Do you have any heroes that you greatly admire?
- What did your high school classmates think you were like?
- What do you do that you wish you could stop doing?
- What would you be doing if time and money weren't an object?

When you are getting together with a person you have spent time with before, review particulars you learned on previous occasions. Maybe you discussed the degree he or she was working on, coaching of a springtime sport, that person's golfing adventures, or that gardening is a beloved hobby. Don't expect to recall these specifics during a pregnant pause—prepare yourself!

The Nonverbal Part of the Conversation

One of my favorite exercises while doing seminars beautifully illustrates the point. I get ten to twelve people in a circle and arbitrarily hand one of them a ball of yarn. That person is to hold onto the end of the yarn, disclose something about him- or herself, and toss the ball of yarn to someone else in the group. The recipient then asks the thrower about what that person said. The recipient then tells something about him- or herself, holds onto the string, and tosses the ball of yarn to the next person. This continues until everyone has had the ball.

I love this exercise because the participants discover several things. First, since they don't know when they'll receive the ball, they pay attention to what everyone else says. Paying attention is the only way they'll be able to ask intelligent questions. Second, they learn to focus on asking appropriate, related questions or making appropriate, related verbal cues.

Asking appropriate questions and making appropriate comments is one of the easiest ways to keep conversations chugging seamlessly along. Third, they pay attention to body language, because the person talking always makes eye contact prior to throwing, so that the ball can be anticipated. If the speaker doesn't make eye contact or the listener isn't paying attention, the conversation ends abruptly with a noticeable thud—*somebody dropped the ball!*

Advance planning and focus help ensure that the ball doesn't get dropped. If you are at an event, such as a luncheon, at which you will spend a considerable amount of time with the same group, be prepared to move beyond icebreakers and initial conversation-starters. You'll need to be able to engage in longer conversations, so you need more topics. This needn't be difficult. If you are worried that you'll forget, keep a note pad of ideas in your wallet or purse to peruse just prior to the event.

The one topic that you needn't have a list for is the one you know best—yourself. Out of courtesy to the introverts in the crowd, I have waited until we were well into the book before getting to this point. Regardless of how many appropriate questions you have on hand, sooner or later you need to talk about yourself. But remember, the rules of good conversation require give and take. If you only ask questions, your conversational partner will resent the lack of parity. Each person needs to tell about him or herself. Now this may be a stretch for some, just as it used to be for me. Along the way, I have discovered that most people who are reticent to talk about themselves fear one or both of these:

- They worry that their lives are much too ordinary to be interesting.
- They do not want to appear self-centered or conceited.

Ordinary People

Guess what? Most of us are doing ordinary things just endeavoring to live our lives in the best way we can. Most of us are concerned about paying bills, educating kids, our favorite teams winning championships, getting promotions, caring for elderly parents, taking occasional vacations, having time for hobbies, relaxing now and then, and so forth. Even those of us doing extraordinary things are more alike than we are different, and our commonality as human beings opens the door for connections and conversations.

Everyone has extraordinary things happen to them that make for excellent conversations. Everyone I know has had an extraordinary experience of one kind or another. There's a hilarious event, a once-in-a-lifetime vacation, a ridiculous moment, an exciting accomplishment, a hair-raising-happy-ending tale, an uncanny coincidence, or an incredible adventure living in your memory bank, just waiting to be shared. Find it and bring it out! Almost anything can be a conversation in the making.

Limelight Etiquette

There are a few rules to remember as you gradually step into the limelight. You will do fine when you follow this advice—no one is lurking about with a hook looking to pull you "offstage." First, disclose information about yourself that is comfortable and uncontroversial. Lead with easy, positive, and light information. Building trust and intimacy over time creates friendships. As previously mentioned, having a conversation is a little like peeling an onion—you want to proceed in layers, matching the level of intimacy shared by your conversational partner.

For instance, suppose your conversational sidekick has just confessed that, after a long holdout, the realities of being parents of kids in sports caused her and her husband to buy a van to cart them around. This does not open the door for you to say that you've been recently diagnosed with breast cancer. However, if the conversation were taking place at "The Race for the Cure," and you were wearing a pink ribbon indicating that you were a cancer survivor, it would be acceptable to discuss breast cancer. Your choice of conversational material needs to be appropriate to the occasion and to the depth of rapport and intimacy established.

I was recently at a luncheon, sitting at one of those round tables with seven other people I had never met. We came to a lull in the conversation that instantly made everyone decide it was time to look at his or her pager for messages. I jumped in with a story about a vacation that my family had taken over spring break. I said, "We went on a Club Med vacation in Mexico last spring and had a great time. It was so hassle-free I couldn't believe it. Since you pay a flat fee for everything, I didn't have to fish for money every time the kids wanted sodas. They just went and got them. It seemed so effortless, and there were activities for all of us."

My vacation story accomplished three things that rejuvenated the conversation. First, I told something about myself, giving others the opportunity to feel more connected to me. Increasing that comfort level stimulates conversation. Second, I offered a new topic that gave material for the others to use. Third, it gave my tablemates the chance to share their own experiences. Conversation sprang to life immediately as others jumped in with questions, stories, and vacation plans of their own.

You aren't limited to talking about events and experiences. You can share feelings, opinions about books you've read, restaurants you've visited, and movies you've seen. For instance, I was at an awards banquet talking with a gentleman. He said, "I'm really nervous being here. My wife had to go away on business so I'm here alone and I don't know anyone else." I talked with him about how nervous I used to be at social functions. That brief interchange helped calm him and we went on to converse at length about a variety of topics.

While there is an infinite list of acceptable conversation topics at public venues, there is also a short list of subjects that are generally off-limits. If you are unsure about a subject's appropriateness and hesitate before bringing it up, it's probably better left unspoken. When unsure, I always invoke the old math axiom my algebra teacher taught me, "When in doubt, leave it out." Avoid any area that is likely to offend your conversation partner.

Speak No Evil

Barring exceptional circumstances, avoid these often-controversial topics that can stop a conversation in its tracks:

- Stories of questionable taste.
- Gossip.
- Personal misfortunes, particularly current ones.
- How much things cost!
- Controversial subjects when you know the other person stands opposite to you on the issues.
- Health (yours or theirs). The exception is when you're talking with someone who obviously has a new cast, crutches, or bandage. In that situation, the apparent temporary medical apparatus is free information. If you skirt the issue it's a bit like having an elephant in your living-room and ignoring it.
- Anything negative.

Playing Four Square

Keeping a conversation rolling is not unlike the old playground game of Four Square. You must pass the ball among all the players and keep the ball in-bounds for play to continue. This requires focusing on the ball at all times and passing it around. Some of the people in your group may be reluctant to receive the ball for the same reasons that you may have been—they're shy, feel like their lives are ordinary, don't enjoy the attention, or something similar. It's up to you to help them or the game will fall apart.

Help Someone Feel Good Not Only About Him- or Herself but About You as Well—*Give a Sincere Compliment*

One of the easiest ways to start or keep a conversation going is to compliment another person. A true compliment helps the other person feel good not only about him or herself but about you as well. It enhances rapport and makes conversation easier. The key is that your compliment be genuine, so select something you can truly support. No matter what you choose, it will be one of three things: appearance, possessions, or behavior. Mark Twain said that a good compliment lasted him 60 days!

Years ago, I had a conversation with my good friend Karen about plans for my wedding. I told her that, for a period of time, I had been dating two men—Ben and Steve. She invited me to tell her about both of them. So I said, "Ben has a great sense of humor. He's the life of the party. He dresses like a million dollars…. He's a great golfer and an all around wonderful guy."

Karen could hardly contain herself, she was so excited. She said, "He sounds like a dream. I'm so happy that you're marrying him."

"I'm not," I replied. "I'm marrying Steve.

Karen was speechless. Finally, she collected herself and said, "Well, Debra, Ben sounds like a prince. Why are you marrying Steve?"

"Because he makes me feel so special by all the wonderful things he says about me. And you know what? He means every one of them!"

The power in a sincere compliment is enormous. There is nothing that makes people feel more special than to have their finer traits noted and appreciated.

The Perfect Compliment

You can compliment others on a new hairstyle, an item of clothing, a piece of jewelry, or their physical appearance. However, not all compliments are created equal. A good compliment acknowledges the object of admiration: "That's a nice sweater you're wearing," or "What an unusual tie." An excellent, top-of-the-line compliment goes beyond that to give *conversational material* by expounding on *why* you like the item. For example, you might elaborate on the sweater by saying, "I love your sweater. That shade really enhances the color of your eyes." You can turn your appreciation of a good-looking tie into a more powerful compliment by saying, "That's a great tie. Its unusual design really sets it apart. I always enjoy it when men make fashion statements with their ties."

Perhaps you are with someone who has no fashion sense whatsoever and you have no appreciation for her taste in clothing, makeup, or accessories. Fear not—you may do better in complimenting her on a possession such as her home, an elegant fountain pen, a new car, or even a coffee mug. A good compliment would be "You have a lovely home." Turn that into state-of-the-art appreciation by saying, "Your home is lovely. I really like all the photos you have—they personalize your home and give it a lot of warmth." Instead of saying, "This is a great cup of coffee," consider, "I love the richness of Indonesian Sumatra, and this is a great-size mug."

Last, but not least, you can notice someone else's behavior. This is the best way to converse with kids. Instead of noticing when they do something wrong, celebrate positive behavior. It not only reinforces the desirable behavior, it'll go a long way toward furthering communication with them and deepening your bonds. Kids are not the only ones who appreciate behavioral compliments. Adults can really open up in the wake of such acknowledgment. It is rare and treasured.

I know a realtor who took a couple house-hunting one Sunday. She drove them all over town and probably showed them over thirty houses. They went in and out of neighborhoods in town, in the suburbs, the works. After six hours, they had completely run out of things to say and still hadn't found a single house that the couple was even remotely considering. The realtor was tired and just about out of ideas.

Then she said, "I really admire that you know exactly what you want. You're not going to settle for something that you don't want and then possibly be unhappy with your choice later." That one compliment got the couple charged up again and they were able to find a new topic of conversation to get them happily through the day, even though they didn't locate their dream house that Sunday.

Other behavioral compliments include comments like:

- I appreciate how organized you are for our meetings. It makes it easy to get the work done.
- It must have taken a lot of courage to change careers during your peak success. I really admire that.
- You have an amazing amount of determination. I think it's remarkable that you set aside time to successfully train for a marathon. Congratulations!
- I know you are concerned about having this procedure done; it's great that you have the courage to do it anyway.
- You certainly have a positive attitude; it is a pleasure to work with you.
- You manage to run such an organized home, even with four children!

Again, the ticket to a successful pat on the back is that you offer it sincerely. You may find that the person you are complimenting has difficulty receiving the praise. He or she may try to neutralize the compliment by denying it or feel obligated to return a compliment. If that happens, reaffirm your sincerity and move on to another subject.

Adding FORM and Substance

Besides complimenting the other person, another way to draw a reluctant participant into a conversation is to toss him or her the ball by asking a question. In addition to the icebreakers back in Chapter Two, there are four categories of questions that are effective in social situations. I use the acronym *FORM* to remember them:

*F*amily—	Tell me about your family." Does everyone live in the area?" What do you like best about being a father or mother, son or aunt, etc.?
*O*ccupation—	What got you into your current job/business? How did you come up with that idea? What are some of the toughest challenges in your field? If you could change one thing about your job/business, what would it be? How has the Internet impacted your business or industry?

*R*ecreation—	What do you do for fitness?
	What kinds of things does your family do for fun?
	How do you spend your leisure time?
	What's been your favorite vacation?
*M*iscellaneous—	Have you seen any good movies lately?
	What do you think about _____(news event)?
	Are you reading anything you really enjoy?
	What do you think about the economy?

No matter what topic of conversation you choose, being authentic is paramount. If you are not genuinely interested in what the other person is saying, no amount of preparation will save you from a doomed conversation. Interest in someone else cannot be faked. If you cannot muster any enthusiasm for the dialogue, politely excuse yourself and make your way to another approachable person.

The March of Progress

You are now about two-thirds of the way through this book. You are becoming more familiar with tips and techniques to make you an excellent conversationalist. This is now a good time to reflect on how far you have come in the practice of these skills and to identify the opportunities for improvement that lay before you. Look at yourself in the mirror and answer with an honest *Yes* or *No* to the following statements:

- I'm conscious of taking turns in conversations so that I can find out about others and help them get to know me.
  ___Yes ___No

- I have participated in at least one activity to meet people and develop new business friendships.
  ___Yes ___No

- I have used my contacts to help at least two people find new jobs or hook up with potential customers and clients.
  ___Yes ___No

- I have given information to someone for other networking purposes. ___Yes ___No

- I go to at least two functions a month where I can meet people in my profession/industry or potential decision-makers. ___Yes ___No

- If another person is friendly to me, I find it easy to be friendly back. However, more and more, I'm the one who is friendly first—who takes the initiative. I don't just wait for people to approach me. ___Yes ___No

- When someone asks, "What's new?" instead of saying, "Not much," I often talk about something exciting in my life. ___Yes ___No

How did you do? If you're like me and have some nos, you probably still have some work to do. It takes effort and practice to change habits. I suggest that you write down one statement reflecting what you want to conquer. Focus on that one goal until you feel comfortable, and then move on to the next. Stay focused and it won't take long!

"During the course of your daily conversations, do your best not to add your name to the eight 'Conversational Criminals' Most Wanted List."

—Debra Fine

-8-

Crimes and Misdemeanors

*"Chances are, unless you are impersonating
Mother Teresa, you have a conversational weakness that
could land you on 'The Most Wanted' List...."*
—Debra Fine—

I travel quite a bit, and one of the biggest trends I've seen is an increase in "assault on a conversation with a deadly weapon." I've been victimized myself a couple of times. The people doing this are "armed and dangerous" and, if they enter your dialogue, you are at serious risk of witnessing the torturous murder of your conversation. Stay on your toes; these people are cleverly disguised. They can orchestrate several costume changes at a single event and impersonate people in every profession. If you sense danger, stay calm. Be on the lookout for these renegades. One further cautionary note: Often, the worst offender is staring at us in the mirror.

I've decided it's time to get more assertive in preventing conversational crimes. I've done an extensive investigation into this phenomenon and have organized the "killers" into eight classifications. During the course of your daily conversations, do your best not to add *your* name to the eight "Conversational Criminals" Most Wanted List:

1. The Interrogator
2. The Braggart

3. The One-Upper
4. The Monopolizer
5. The Interrupter
6. The Poor Sport
7. The Know-It-All
8. The Advisor

Here are some "crime-fighting" techniques to keep each type of "Conversational Criminal" honest so they don't take advantage of you:

The Interrogator

This interrogator definitely does not have the people's interests at heart. He or she can be seen stalking casual conversations and pulling people aside for interrogation. You will immediately recognize their unmistakable modus operandi because they fire question after question at you, like a machine gun in the jungle. "What do you do for a living?" "Where are you from?" "You married?" "Got any kids?" "Lived here long?" "How long have you been on the job?" "What's your mother's maiden name?"

The interrogator relentlessly assaults the other party with a barrage of questions. The interrogator leaves no opportunity for the "prisoner" to even offer a confession of any kind. The prisoner is not allowed to expand beyond a simple answer— offer additional evidence, ask questions, or even have a glass of water. Forget about getting a phone call or a lawyer. The prisoner is forced to give staccato answers just to keep pace. That person is held in custody at the whim of the interrogator. When the interrogator completes the questioning, he or she unceremoniously dumps the prisoner and moves on to round up another suspect.

The interrogator errs by walloping the prisoner with an endless barrage of questions. The interrogator would be much more successful by asking open-ended questions that require more extensive answers. The prisoner would cough up plenty of information effortlessly if given the opportunity. The interrogator also makes the mistake of settling for one- or two-word answers and failing to dig deeper. The interrogator could have uncovered motives, alibis, opportunities, and background information that would have been quite helpful in his or her quest for conversation had he or she asked appropriate, probing questions.

The interrogator is characterized by exceptional nervousness. Help this person out by taking control of the conversational ball. Ask an open-ended question. Follow up—dig deeper and use verbal listening cues. For instance, ask what he or she does for a living. Follow up with questions about what is entailed in that kind of occupation and how that person got into it. Become the host and attend to the interrogator's comfort. This allows you to slow down the conversation. Eventually, you will be able to get into a rhythm of a nice back and forth, easy volley with the conversational ball.

The Braggart

This convict made his way onto "The Most Wanted List" by executing a series of conversational mass murders all over the nation. He frequently appears during periods of self-disclosure. He will boast of his accomplishments, embellish the truth, and brag about feats mighty and small in a very self-aggrandizing manner. He usually makes no attempt to go incognito; so arrogant is he. His goal is to gain status in the eyes of those present, so he welcomes an audience. The bigger the group, the more bravado he feels. He has been known to kill multiple conversations with a single appearance.

His trademark is that he will always relate all of his accomplishments. He made a killing on the stock market. He'll tell how he outwitted the financial experts by choosing a long shot that paid off big. Of course, his child is the captain of the baseball team, and pro scouts are recruiting this unsuspecting kid. You'll be spared no details. Perhaps he just bought a top-of-the-line car. He can't imagine why everyone else doesn't do the same. He always has an "I'm the king of the world" story to tell.

The braggart's sister, Braggarta, is equally lethal, although she prefers single encounters with people she knows. She usually prefers to do her boasting in a more personal way. She tends to speak conspiratorially to members of her inner circle. She leaves it to them to spread the word of her greatness to unknown parties. Braggarta never directly discloses her greatness to strangers. She lets them find out from her clique of confidantes who are charged with telling others. While strangers are not required to bow to Braggarta, it is expected that they will be suitably impressed.

She will very quietly tell her inner circle about her new designer kitchen and how much it cost. She'll tell them about a smashing vacation on the French Riviera that everyone else must take. In fact, she'll give you the name of her travel agent just so you can perfectly replicate the trip.

The only hope of stopping a conversational murder orchestrated by the braggart and Braggarta is to bring the conversation back to more general topics, such as current events. You can also refocus the conversation on your own life, telling about something you are currently doing. There is no point in going toe-to-toe with either of them, because it is impossible to directly stave off their boastfulness. The only tactic that could work is for you to redirect the conversation.

The One-Upper

Members of this longstanding conversational crime family are first cousins to the braggart and his sister. These folks generally come from a patriarchal lineage, as women usually don't have the same interest in this mode of murder. While the one-uppers generally do not brag first, they always top someone else's story. They seem to be completely unaware that they have offended others by constantly trumping their stories. Sometimes the one-uppers genuinely believe they are showing compassion and demonstrating excellent listening skills by topping others' tales.

You know the scene. Your colleague Brian is looking for a new job and you inquire about how the search is progressing. As soon as Brian offers an update, John launches into a tale about his own difficulties on the job, making it seem like unemployment is preferable to his own job woes. Before you know it, the group is talking all about what's going on in the industry, and Brian's job search is lost in the shuffle. His troubles weren't acknowledged. No solutions were offered. No empathy was given. No encouraging words were offered to him. Brian was left feeling like no one really cared about his plight. While John might have thought he was being supportive, he wasn't. He simply diverted attention away from Brian and onto himself.

Women can also be experts at topping another's story but, instead, their approach is often to match someone else. For instance, Rose talks about relationship problems she's having with Mark, and Shelley commiserates by saying, "Honey, I know just what you mean. My Anthony had the nerve to...." The woman who matched the initial woman's story didn't really commiserate. She stole the show. She took the spotlight off the other woman and put it right on herself. She stopped the other woman in the middle of her story.

A particularly troublesome spot for women can be in talking about their kids. Sometimes I have to control myself from jumping in and telling my own kid tales when another woman is telling a story about hers. Instead of enjoying the story she is sharing, I can get sidetracked because her story reminds me of something similar that my kids did at the same age. I get so excited that I just want to jump right in there because I'm exhilarated by the conversation. This is definitely not a stalled conversation—everyone wants the ball! However, it's very deflating to the person telling the original story. Her story is the one that got the group so enthusiastic. It's important to acknowledge that and to enjoy such a great story. There's no need to rush to the next. It's like hurrying through a finely prepared meal—you miss most of the experience in the rush to complete it!

Be aware of one of the most prevalent "one-upping" statements circulating these days: "Been there, done that." In one very short sentence, the person uttering those four words is saying that the story is old news, that there is nothing else to say about that topic. It lets the other person know, in no uncertain terms, that his or her experience is universal, and to spare the rest of us the details of such a boring story. Crimestoppers report that it is tough to topple the one-upper who is quite successful in crushing a conversation to death. Those still standing usually attempt to regroup in a clandestine fashion, to prevent yet another crime.

The Monopolizer

A master of disguise, the monopolizer has managed to infiltrate conversations around the world. Victims are shocked to discover that even a very introverted and shy person can turn out to be a monopolizer. The monopolizer can turn up anywhere, even at the most exclusive of events. That person strikes boldly, seizing the conversation in plain view of all. He or she can enter any conversation and artfully gain control before even a single person can react. There is never any shortage of witnesses to the monopolizer's crimes but, nonetheless, people are initially too captivated to take action. The monopolizer takes the spotlight through self-disclosure and retains it by continuing to "peel the layers of the onion" without regard to whether anyone in the group is feeling any discomfort.

Monopolizers feel justified. They believe they are performing a community service by keeping the conversational ball rolling. Usually shy people who find that the spotlight is rather fun can be the worst offenders.

Instead of hogging the ball, the monopolizer would do well to pass it to someone else in the group. I have a personal rule to never talk for more than five minutes before passing the ball. The challenge is that time flies when we're talking about ourselves! No matter what the topic—how I lost 65 pounds, how I got into business, why my kids are so incredible—the clock is ticking. But when my five minutes are up, I pass the ball on to someone else with an appropriate question or comment. You might adopt a similar rule for yourself as well. Others will appreciate that.

If you are alone with a monopolizer, you have several options to salvage the situation. If you are with your boss, a client, or your mother-in-law, it's usually best to surrender and give the gift of listening. Once in a while you can be successful for brief interludes by changing the topic, using self-disclosure, or asking a prepared question. However, it is impossible to make a monopolizer stop repeating this habitual behavior. You can't change anyone. That person needs to want to change—perhaps realizing that others are just tolerating or avoiding him or her altogether. If your career or your relationship with your extended family is on the line, just surrender and consider it a random act of kindness.

There are occasions when you can momentarily stop a monopolizer. When you are approaching the saturation point, throw out a "white (surrender) flag" as a warning. Just like a racecar driver gets a white flag indicating time constraints, you must throw out one before you can legitimately stop a monopolizer in his or her tracks.

For example, you are in your office and your friend Gary comes by to tell you about his golf game. When you are running out of time, interest, or willpower, you throw out a white flag by saying, "Wow, Gary. That's an amazing round you shot. Before you continue, I need to let you know that in a few minutes I have to get back to preparing the budget." You have politely given Gary the signal that you need to end the conversation shortly. Gary takes another four minutes telling you of his exploits on the twelfth and thirteenth holes. You can now wrap it up by saying, "Well, Gary, that's really something. But I have to take care of the budget right now. Maybe we can catch up another time." You can now turn your attention to your budget without concern. You were gracious and obliging, and gave fair warning that it was time to end the chat.

If you are in a group of three or more, assume the role of host and make an interception. Every year, I get together with some college friends for an evening to catch up. My friend Lori is infamous for her legendary ability to monopolize the conversation. Given my line of work, I feel it incumbent upon myself to help the group and facilitate passing the ball. So I jump in after she's had more than her five minutes on the floor and say, "Lori, that's a great story about Adam's hitting streak. Marilyn, what's been going on with your kids?" Connecting Lori's story about her son to Marilyn's kids lends continuity to the conversation while diplomatically allowing someone else a chance to talk. As Uncle Joe is going on endlessly about his life as an auditor, transition the conversation to someone else. "That sounds tough, Uncle Joe. Cousin Larry, what's going on for you at work?"

Monopolizers have shown that they are candidates for rehabilitation. They can be successful in restoring conversational balance once they realize that talking incessantly is not exactly a favor to everyone else. Remember that, as the host, your goal is not only to get the monopolizer to yield the floor; it is to include others—especially the quiet ones. Invite them into the dialogue with a question or comment directed to them. Even when there isn't a monopolizer involved in the conversation, pass the ball to at least one other person.

The Interrupter

Beware of the interrupter! This villain comes in all shapes, sizes, and haircuts. I've often wondered if the interrupter was prevented from ever finishing a sentence as a kid and is taking out those childhood experiences on society. The interrupter is characterized by high drive, determination to make a point, and a lack of patience. I confess that I have done time as an interrupter. I was convicted for interrupting my husband relentlessly. I was on probation for a while, but after three strikes, I was convicted. My husband is very low-key, and my interruptions caused him a great deal of angst. He understood my temperament and was torn about confronting me. But after I interrupted him one too many times, he demanded relief.

Frequently, he would start to say something and provide rationale for his point. If I didn't agree, I'd jump right in without letting him finish. I didn't want to wait three minutes for him to finish his point—it seemed like an eternity. Most interrupters are like me. We interrupt because we think we know what others are going to say, so let's not waste time. Or we believe that others are wrong and we must hurry to point out the errors of their ways. We may also interrupt because we believe we may forget what we want to share after the other person is done speaking.

However, having already gone through one divorce, I wasn't interested in destroying our near-perfect union with my short attention span and lack of patience. I have since realized that interruptions badly sabotage a good conversation, so I now campaign against them.

There are only two good reasons for interrupting. The first is that you need to exit immediately, for instance, for an emergency. The second is that the topic of conversation is too uncomfortable to bear and you need to change it right away.

Now, you may be thinking, "What if my office or cell phone rings?" Is that a good reason for interrupting a conversation? As a rule, it is best not to answer the phone. If you do, you dishonor the person who is with you. If you're expecting an important call, have the courtesy to tell the person you're talking with that you're expecting such a call. Ask if he or she would mind if you interrupted the conversation and took the call when it came in. This shows respect for the person you are with, and it will go a long way in building the relationship.

The Poor Sport

The poor sport has an unparalleled reputation for conversational suicide. The poor sport will kill his or her own conversation by refusing to play by the rules. A very cunning illusionist, the poor sport changes open-ended questions into closed-ended quips.

Using smoke and mirrors, the poor sport always finds a way to reduce a beautiful question into a simple one-word answer. When asked, "What did you do this weekend?" the poor sport will reply with, "Nothing." The question left plenty of room for the poor sport to select some aspect of the weekend for conversation. Instead, that person starved the conversation by withholding food. The poor sport just doesn't play well with others—he or she ignores the rules, pouts, and quits the game without warning.

Some poor sports simply have never been properly trained; they simply don't know how to ask open-ended questions. With an outreach program, some of them show promise. You can help a poor sport by answering a closed-end question as if it had been open-ended. For instance, if a poor sport asks, "How was your weekend?" don't just say, "Great. What about yours?" Instead, teach by example. Offer, "Great. We took the kids skiing and it was a perfect day. The only glitch was that Mike took a bad spill, but he's okay now." You have helped the poor sport. You have given him or her lots of material with which he or she can ask a related question, keeping the conversation from entering a slow demise. You've offered information about yourself that can help bridge the gap and create conversation. One cautionary note: It is very easy to become a monopolizer in the presence of a poor sport. Exercise restraint and keep tossing the ball back to the other person. Share information that will contribute to the conversation, but don't steal the show!

The Know-It-All

These nasty criminals will mow you down with arrogance and condescension. They think they know everything, and they tell you so. They just knew that the stock market was going to take a dive or hit a high. In fact, they knew that the election would be close, that the winter was going to be brutal, and on and on. There is just no end to what they know. And since they know they are always right, they see no point in soliciting other opinions. If someone offers one, they cut that person down without hesitation. In seconds they can silence an entire group because no one wants to risk humiliation at the hands of the know-it-all. Watch out for the person who has absolutely no interest in anyone else's opinions but his or her own.

Be careful if you flaunt your opinions. Make sure that others realize you are only offering your personal opinion about what works for you. There is one simple question that, when used properly, prevents anyone from becoming a know-it-all. It is this four-word query: "What is your opinion?"

The Advisor

The advisor always leaves a calling card at the scene of the crime. He or she is readily identifiable by that person's endless array of solutions to everyone else's problems. This person is a veritable expert at everything. There isn't any problem the advisor can't offer a solution for—even when no one wants one! Unsolicited advice is offered generously, and without charge.

Despite a generous nature, the advisor is a true outlaw who decimates a perfectly good chat by meddling. The truth is, most people don't want advice—they want empathy and compassion. When the advisor rides in on a white horse to save the day, the very person he or she is trying to rescue is minimized. The presumption is that in hearing a tiny snippet of another's dilemma, the advisor has an intimate understanding of the problem and knows the perfect solution. He or she would do much better digging deeper to learn more about the issue and offering empathetic support instead of unsolicited solutions.

The advisor is very seductive because of being upbeat, confident, and wanting to help. That's what makes him or her so wily. It is easy to unwittingly emulate that person. Recently, in fact, I did an unintentional impersonation of the advisor and was mortified once I realized it!

I was having lunch with my friend, Bill, who recently received a promotion to manage a large sales territory for a medical supply company. He was talking about the difficulties with a new sales rep: His sales were off, he wasn't making headway, and he was discouraged. Well, I just chimed right in with all the solutions I had for him. I said, "I think the key to success is to sell, sell, sell. Visibility is everything. I just kept knocking on doors till they started opening."

Bill didn't need my advice; he needed my support. He just wanted to talk about his difficulties and share his thoughts. But in giving solutions, I wasn't empathetic; I was presumptuous. Bill did not ask for advice. He wasn't seeking my infinite wisdom—he just wanted an attentive ear. Don't make the same mistake. Give the gift of listening and offer advice only when it's solicited.

Advisors are everywhere. I had an encounter with one on the ski slopes of Colorado. I was in Vail to give a seminar to ski instructors. I decided to ignore my fear of heights and take a skiing lesson to better see how the instructors might benefit from the seminar. I was grouped with a family from Alabama who had never even seen snow before. As the lesson progressed, the instructor noticed how cautiously I was skiing—I was even more reticent than the Alabamans! The instructor decided that I must have had weak quad muscles. He showed me some strengthening exercises to solve that problem.

The real problem, though, was that the advisor/instructor diagnosed the difficulty without even asking me any questions. He had no idea that I am an avid runner; my quad strength is fine, thank you very much! My terror at standing at an altitude of over 11,000 feet practically paralyzed me. Had the advisor bothered to find that out, he could have given me a much more effective skiing lesson. Had he dug deeper, he would have discovered that his premature analysis of my problem was completely incorrect.

Physicians can be among the most notorious advisors. They frequently interrupt the patient and diagnose the problem before the patient has a chance to tell the whole story. Frequently, the patient doesn't get to the heart of the matter until the doctor has his hand on the doorknob, about to exit the room. If only the doctor would just sit and listen to the patient completely before rendering an opinion, the appointment would be much more successful. Each would enjoy reduced frustration and a better outcome!

A Crime-Free Conversation

These eight criminals can bleed the life right out of a conversation. Sure, there are criminal wannabes too. Most of those folks are petty criminals specializing in misdemeanors that can hurt a good gab session, but they can't kill it. You have the skills to deal with those kinds of infractions. However, when you recognize one of "The Most Wanted," exercise extreme caution. Even the most vigilant conversationalist can still get ambushed. You can even take down your own conversation because, the truth is, we each have a rap sheet. I, myself, am a chronic interrupter if I don't police myself. Chances are that unless you are impersonating Mother Teresa, you have a conversational weakness that could land you on "The Most Wanted" list if you're not careful. Be on the lookout for your own criminal activity, for you may be aiding and abetting the murder of a good conversation.

Even if you take the high road and have a clean conversational record, you never know when you'll find yourself with a convicted felon on the loose, slaughtering a perfectly good conversation. Sometimes, there's nothing that can be done except to preserve your own safety with a quick getaway. Knowing that, it behooves you to have several escape routes planned so you can exit in a hurry, if need be. Fear not—I wouldn't leave you in harm's way. Your escape hatch is waiting.

"Be on the lookout for your own criminal activity, for you may be aiding and abetting the murder of a good conversation."

—Debra Fine

"The cardinal rule of the exit is that when you depart, you do what you said you were going to do. If you said goodbye to Joanne by telling her you were going to see the exhibits, then go see the exhibits. Don't chance hurting the relationship you have with your previous partner by failing to get to your next destination."

—Debra Fine

-9-

The Graceful Exit

"Ending a conversation by showing appreciation for the interchange is a great way to leave on a positive note."
—Debra Fine—

Whether you are trying to escape from a convicted conversation killer or just want to circulate more, there are ways to artfully exit a conversation without offending the other person.

I find that many people remain in a conversation longer than they need to for two reasons: (1) They feel trapped, especially if it's just a two-person dialogue, or (2) they are so comfortable that they don't want to leave. If you are at a party, a meeting, or another gathering, and your goal is to meet people, you need to find the courage to leave a comfortable conversation with someone you know in order to accomplish your goals. Done properly, an authentic farewell will actually enhance your relationship.

When you prepare to leave a conversation, recall why you originally connected with your conversational partner, and then bring the conversation back to that topic. Doing so will allow you to make a meaningful connection and then take your leave easily. For instance, I was at an open house arranged by a large corporation. Before I left my conversational partner, I said, "Tom, it's been wonderful talking with you about the changes impacting the healthcare industry. I need to catch up with another client before she leaves. Thanks for sharing your expertise." Tom returned the compliment, we shook hands, and I headed toward my client while Tom went in another direction.

Notice that I didn't make excuses for my leaving. I didn't say I had to call the babysitter or that I needed to return a page. That age-old adage "Honesty is the best policy," really works. It's important to retain your composure and courteously state your reason for departing. Even if you despised the conversation and are anxious to leave, be tactful as you go. Here are some diplomatic ways to make your exit:

- I need to go see the exhibits.
- I want to go talk to the speaker.
- I'm going to circulate and meet some of the new members.
- I want to see if there are any other people from my industry here today.
- I need to speak with the membership chairperson before she leaves.
- I promised myself that I'd meet three new people before I leave this evening.
- I want to meet some other potential clients this morning.
- I want to get around and say hello to everyone at this meeting/party/event.

These exit lines are successful because they put the focus directly on you. You clearly state that the reason you are leaving the conversation is that *you* need to do something. There is no mistaking the fact that you are endeavoring to accomplish a specific agenda. By highlighting your own goals, you take the burden off your conversational partner. He or she now knows that your need to move on has nothing to do with the quality of the time you just spent with that person.

The cardinal rule of the exit is that when you depart, you do what you said you were going to do. If you said goodbye to Joanne by telling her you were going to see the exhibits, then go see the exhibits. If you allow yourself to get side-tracked en route to your new destination, you run the risk of insulting your former partner. For instance, if Vince stops you on your way to the exhibits, do not stay and talk. Instead, say, "Vince, it's good to see you. I was just on my way to the exhibits. Would you like to join me or can I catch up with you afterward?" If you make the mistake of getting immersed in a conversation with Vince, all Joanne sees is that you didn't go to the exhibits. She now presumes that you were never headed there, and that your true goal was to just end the conversation. You now have a tarnished reputation, an upset person, and other possible unintended consequences. Don't chance hurting the relationship you have with your previous partner by failing to get to your next destination.

Taking Care of Business

Staying focused on your own agenda makes your conversations much more productive than if you are just casually mingling with whomever walks through the door. You will have questions prepared and, preferably, a cast of characters in mind that you'd like to meet. Keeping track of your own progress toward accomplishing your objectives will help you gain the motivation to exit one conversation and get involved in another. It also provides you with a number of getaway lines.

You can invoke your partner's help in exiting by getting a referral or asking for business. For instance, you've been talking to Shelly for about fifteen minutes, and you need to see some other people before the party ends. Shelly can actually help you do that if you let her. You say, "Shelly, I've been having trouble with the graphics package on my Mac at home. Do you know anyone here who uses this program on a PC?" Shelly will either give you a lead to the appropriate person or she'll say she doesn't know anyone with that program. Either way, you've created a clean break. If Shelly can't help you, you simply thank her, tell her that you really need to find someone, and say goodbye. It's really that easy. Don't invent a problem, though, just to end a conversation. Mentally check your agenda and ask for a referral to someone connected to assisting you in forwarding your goals.

Suppose you want to find some prospective clients or associates to expand your business. If you went to a gathering with such an agenda, you need to verbalize it to accomplish it. You can do this easily without putting your conversational partner on the spot. You could simply say, "Patrick, do you know anyone who might be interested in increasing his or her income without jeopardizing what that person is now doing?"

A question like that provides you with a couple of good results. First, it lets the other party know, in a very unobtrusive way, that you are looking for an ambitious person. Who knows? Patrick himself just might be interested. The second result is that you've opened up channels with other people. Patrick may say, "Jim, over there by the door is Jack. He is a real winner and just may be interested." You can then graciously leave the conversation and head over toward someone who may be interested in your opportunity. You easily introduce yourself to Jim saying, "I was just talking with Patrick and he told me that you're a real winner." You have an introduction and a topic of conversation with no effort or angst! You may even get a new associate or client out of the deal.

Don't hesitate to ask for business or referrals as you take your leave from a conversation. Everyone at a business meeting has an agenda—and virtually everyone is always looking for new business. There is no shortage of ways to ask for referrals or business. The following are some methods to take care of business; try some of them out and tailor a couple to fit your needs and personality:

- Can you recommend anyone who needs a _____? I'd appreciate the referral.
- Can you suggest anyone with whom I could speak about _____?
- Who do you know that might be able to help me with _____?
- I had hoped to meet someone who is interested in _____. Do you know anyone like that?
- Who else here could I speak to about joining the ____ committee?
- I'm looking for a _____ job. Are you aware of any openings?

These techniques are not unique to business situations. You can easily adapt them to social events as well. Here are some examples:

- I'd like to find someone who is interested in hiking or has info on hiking groups. Do you know whether anyone here can help me?
- Do you know anyone here that's new to the area?
- I'm looking for someone interested in volunteer activities. Can you suggest someone?

The Changing of the Guard

A time-honored tradition of leaving a conversation is by executing a changing of the guard. When a new person enters the group and begins talking to one or two people, one or more other people may bow out. It is a quick and easy escape used by people all the time. The downside of this technique is that it facilitates *only* an exit, but if you are just looking for the nearest emergency exit, this can be your ticket.

A slight variation on the theme is to take your conversational partner with you as you exit. This can be done even when it's just the two of you talking. You introduce your conversational party to someone who can render assistance to him or her. This transition is easily made with statements like these:

- I'd like to introduce you to an associate of mine who's in your field. Let's see if she's around.
- Matt is a great guy with an interesting history. I'd like to introduce you two to each other.
- Let's go meet the speaker.
- I see my friend Jennifer is here. Let's go say hi.
- Let's circulate. I promised myself I'd meet some new people here.
- Let's go get some dinner.

Inviting your partner to join you on your way to another destination is a very gracious and considerate way to exit. You are still focused on your own agenda, but you haven't left your associate behind. Reverse the situation and think about the other person inviting you to join him or her. It's a perfect opportunity to get introduced to another person, or you can gracefully decline, feeling positive about the offer.

A Little Appreciation Goes a Long Way

Ending a conversation by showing appreciation for the interchange is a great way to leave on a positive note. Thanking others for their time, expertise, or the sheer joy of their conversational participation is always welcome. You emanate poise and self-confidence when you bid adieu by expressing your gratitude and praising your partner in some way. This is accomplished in much the same way as using a compliment to move a conversation along, and the same rule applies: Be genuine. Done sincerely, offering gratitude will produce a wave of goodwill and a positive association with your name. Appreciation is a compliment with closure. You and your partner separate, feeling good about each other. Some ways to do this are to say:

- It was wonderful to see you and hear about the convention.
- I've really enjoyed talking with you about your new business.
- I appreciate your willingness to share your expertise.
- Thank you for the delightful conversation.
- I'm so glad you introduced me to the subject of ____. It's very interesting.
- It's nice to meet someone involved in ____.
- It was so thoughtful of you to introduce me to ___. Thanks.
- I appreciate your effort to include me in the conversation. It's a challenge being new and you made it easier for me.

Remember to end the conversation the same way you began it—with a smile and a handshake. Even if you have to get up and walk around the table to do so, make sure you do it. You make a lasting impression when you seal a conversation with a handshake. Just that fleeting hand-to-hand moment enhances the rapport you've worked so hard to establish. Just melting away into the crowd discredits your integrity and intentions. The end of the conversation represents the last opportunity to establish a connection with someone. Capitalize on it with enthusiasm!

Parting Is Such Sweet Sorrow

If you've met someone with whom you'd like to further a relationship, the best way to exit is to ask to see that person again. Assume the responsibility of issuing the invitation regardless of your gender. If you are female, do not think that you have to wait for the male to make the offer—regardless of whether it's a business or social engagement. I'm not in the business of dispensing advice for singles so please don't construe this as such. This is about using conversations successfully to create win-win relationships and accomplish your goals. If your goal is to meet a new person and cultivate a relationship, then do so. Gender is immaterial as long as your behavior is appropriate.

Muster your moxie and just do it. Sure, you'll feel a bit out of your comfort zone, but the only way you can pick the fruit is to go out on a limb. Realize that if you get turned down, it's not a statement about you—it's about the other person and his or her agenda. That individual doesn't know you well enough to draw any meaningful conclusions about you. Remember my friend Rex—his shyness was why he didn't invite me to sit with him. If someone turns you down, you can't possibly know the reason unless it is offered. Here are some ways to invite the other person to continue the relationship:

- I don't want to monopolize your time this evening. Can we arrange to meet later?
- Will I see you at the next meeting?
- I'll be thinking of you during your ____. May I call you when you get back?
- I'd enjoy spending some time with you. Can I phone you to set up a convenient time?
- I'll drop off that article we discussed at your office next week. I'll phone you and schedule a time.
- I'd like to rehash what we did in class tonight. Would you like to join me for a cup of coffee?
- I enjoyed working out with you. Do you want to meet next week and do it again?

- I hope we can do business together soon. May I call you in the coming days to determine your level of interest?

Before you leave a conversation, have a clear destination in mind. You don't necessarily need to head to another conversation. Feel free to get something to eat, get a fresh beverage, call the sitter and check on the kids, use the restroom, or even take a stroll around the room. Movement attracts attention, so make sure you don't look lost. If your former conversation partner perceives that you are aimlessly wandering, he or she may feel insulted that you prefer your own company to theirs.

Because the manner in which you exit a conversation leaves a lasting impression, develop finesse at doing graceful departures. There is nothing mysterious about these techniques—a degree in rocket science is not needed. They are common-sense tips, but they are not common practice. Practice frequently until you can comfortably disengage yourself from conversations using a variety of methods. Acquiring this skill will undoubtedly improve your overall confidence and presence. That enhanced composure will, in turn, make you an ever-more inviting conversational partner.

"*Always take the risk and assume the responsibility of starting a conversation and keeping it going.*"

—Debra Fine

-10-

The Conversational Ball Is in Your Court!

*"Be able to succinctly tell others
what you do in a few short sentences."*
—Debra Fine—

Here are fifty tips you can review before any event, occasion, or interview. Always take the risk and assume the responsibility of starting a conversation and keeping it going. Review the following, then go to whatever meeting, luncheon, party, or other gathering awaits you and seize the day!

50 Ways to Start and Fuel a Conversation

1. Be the first to smile and say hello.
2. Introduce yourself to others first.
3. Take risks and anticipate success.
4. Remember to use your sense of humor. Have fun with the process.
5. Practice different ways of starting conversations.
6. Make an extra effort to remember people's names.
7. Always ask a person's name if you've forgotten it.
8. Be curious and interested in learning about others.
9. Tell others about the important events in your life. Don't wait for them to draw it out of you.

10. Demonstrate that you are listening by restating your conversational partner's comments in another way—paraphrase.
11. Communicate enthusiasm and excitement about things and life in general.
12. Go out of your way to meet new people wherever you are.
13. Accept a person's right to be an individual with different ideas and beliefs.
14. Let the natural you come out when talking to others.
15. Be able to succinctly tell others what you do in a few short sentences.
16. Re-introduce yourself to someone who is likely to have forgotten your name.
17. Be ready to tell others something interesting or challenging about what you do.
18. Be aware of open and closed body language.
19. Go find the approachable person, smile, make eye contact, and offer a handshake.
20. Pleasantly greet both people that you see regularly and those you don't.
21. Seek common interests, goals, and experiences with the people you meet.
22. Make an effort to help people whenever you can.
23. Let others play the experts.
24. Be open to answering common ritualistic questions.
25. Be enthusiastic and inquisitive about other people's interests.
26. Balance the time between giving and receiving information.
27. Be able to talk about a variety of topics and subjects.
28. Keep up to date on current events and issues that affect our lives.
29. Express your feelings, opinions, and emotions to others.
30. Use "I" when you speak about your own feelings and personal things, rather than "you."
31. Visually show others that you are enjoying your conversations with them.

32. To further relationships, be ready to issue invitations to others to join you for other events and activities.
33. Find ways to keep in touch with the friends and acquaintances you meet.
34. Seek out others' opinions.
35. Look for the positive in those you meet.
36. Start and end your conversations with the people's names and handshakes or warm greetings.
37. Take the time to be friendly with your neighbors and co-workers.
38. Let others know that you would like to get to know them better.
39. Ask others about things they have told you in previous conversations.
40. Listen carefully for free information.
41. Be ready to ask open-ended questions to learn more.
42. Change the topic of conversation when it has run its course.
43. Always search for the things that really get the other person excited.
44. Compliment others about what they own or are wearing, doing, or saying.
45. Encourage others to talk to you by sending out positive signals.
46. Make an effort to see and talk to people you could enjoy.
47. When you tell a story, present the main point first, and then add the supporting details afterwards.
48. Include everyone in the group in conversation whenever possible.
49. Look for signs of boredom or lack of interest from your listener.
50. Prepare ahead of time for each social or business function.

"During an awkward social gathering, a demanding sales presentation, or a tough interview, casual conversation can turn a challenging situation into a gratifying success. Casual conversation connects us to others, whether the setting is business or social."

—Debra Fine

-11-

Make the Most of Networking and Relationship-Building Opportunities

*"Casual conversation connects us to others
whether the setting is business or social."*
—Debra Fine—

Learn how to make the most of meetings, interviews, and other networking opportunities as well as entertaining clients at conventions, trade shows, and other business-related functions.

Do you dread receptions, banquets, and other work-related social events? Does attending another open house make you want to run inside your house and lock the door? You're not alone. Many of us are apprehensive about entering rooms where we don't know anyone or spending time with people we don't know well. We need to practice keeping conversations going so we are better prepared for such occasions.

For those of us who are business professionals, these occasions represent opportunities to develop business friendships and broaden our networks. Whether it's obvious or not, networking happens all the time.

During an awkward social gathering, a demanding sales presentation, or a tough interview, casual conversation can turn a challenging situation into a gratifying success. Casual conversation connects us to others, whether the setting is business or social.

Most everyone learns required technical skills, but not everyone places importance on conversational skills. The ability to talk easily with anyone is a learned skill—not a personality trait. Acquiring or polishing it will help you develop rapport with people and leave positive impressions that last longer than simple exchanges of business cards.

Here are a few tips business professionals can use to improve their casual conversational skills:

- **Initiate conversations with friendly greetings.** The other people, especially if shy, will be grateful.
- **Introduce yourself.** Act as if you're the host and introduce new arrivals to your conversational partner or partners.
- **Smile first and always shake hands when you meet someone.** This helps you establish yourself as a personable, respectful, kind individual.
- **Take your time during introductions.** Make an extra effort to remember names, and use them frequently in conversations. Note and use the names as shared with you. For example, if someone introduces herself as Katherine, use that name rather than a nickname version.
- **Maintain eye contact during every conversation.** Many of us when in a group of three or more people look around in the hope that others will maintain eye contact on our behalves. People only feel listened to when we are looking at them.
- **Get somebody to talk** about why he or she is attending the event, and you are on your way to engaging that person in conversation.

- **Show an interest in everyone you talk to.** The more interest you show, the wiser and more attractive you become to others.
- **Listen carefully** for information that can keep the conversation going.
- **Remember, people want to be with people who make them feel special,** not people who act as if they are special. Take responsibility to help people you talk to feel as if they're the only people in the room.
- **Play the conversation game.** When someone asks, "How's business?" or "What's going on?" answer with more than "Not much." Tell more about yourself so others can learn more about you.
- **Be careful with business acquaintances.** You wouldn't want to open a conversation with: "How's your job at _____?" What if that person just got fired or laid off? Be careful when you're asking about an acquaintance's spouse or special friend; you could regret it.
- **Don't act like you're an "interrogator."** Questions like "What do you do?," "Are you married?," "Do you have children?," and "Where are you from?" lead to dead-end conversations.
- **Be aware of body language.** Nervous or ill-at-ease people are uncomfortable to be around. Act confident and comfortable, even if you're not, until you become so.
- **Be prepared.** Spend a few minutes before an anticipated event preparing to talk easily about three topics. They will come in handy when you find yourself in the middle of an awkward moment or seated at a table of eight where everyone is playing with his or her food.
- **Show an interest in your conversational partner's opinion too.** You're not the only person who has opinions about funding the space program or what will happen to the stock market.
- **Stop a conversation monopolist in his or her tracks.** If possible, wait for the person to take a breath or to pause,

then break in with a comment about the topic. After that, immediately lead the conversation in the direction in which you want it to go.

- **Be prepared with exit lines.** Remember, you do need to move around and meet others. That's the only way you can more ahead.
- **Don't melt from a conversation.** Make a positive impression by shaking hands and saying goodbye as you leave.

Meeting someone new involves risk, but it's well worth it. As long as you keep looking for new people to meet and show an interest in others, you can make more friends and enjoy lively conversations.

"*Meeting some-one new involves risk, but it's well worth it. As long as you keep looking for new people to meet and show an interest in others, you can make more friends and enjoy more lively conversations.*"

—Debra Fine

"*Whether you want to land a new job, enhance your practice, gain listings, increase your billable hours, gain new clients or customers, bring new people into you business, or encourage people to remember you with referrals—always pay attention to the feel-friendly factor. Then enjoy the success that follows.*"

—Debra Fine

-12-

The Feel-Friendly Factor

"Use casual conversation not just to be sociable, but also to put a picture frame around business conversations."
—Debra Fine—

A person will part with money for two reasons: (1) He or she believes you can solve his or her problem, and (2) you can help that person feel friendly toward you in the process.

For example, it's hard to quickly evaluate the expertise of a new dentist, but you know immediately which one helps you feel more comfortable. You can take lessons from a highly qualified ski instructor, but if you feel awkward in his or her silence while riding the chair lift together, you'll switch instructors. When two stores offer the same item at about the same price and the stores are located near each other, where do you buy? You choose the store where the returns are simpler, the people are friendlier, and the appearance is cleaner—where you feel more welcome.

The *feel-friendly factor* underlies every aspect of life. Even in the area of parent-teacher conferences, if your child's teacher delivers negative feedback in a way that shows empathy, not harshness, you're more likely to support the next vote to increase school taxes.

In a front-page story, *USA Today* reported that basketball star Kareem Abdul Jabbar hired a public relations professional to help him get job interviews for coaching positions. Apparently, he's perceived as so aloof, he can't get high schools, colleges, or the pros to talk to him. Similarly, in the work-a-day world, if you want a promotion but come across as aloof or reserved, you'll be overlooked in favor of someone who has warm people skills—skills which encourage others to feel more friendly toward you.

Here's how to build the rapport that leads to success in every business relationship:

- **Use casual conversation not just to be sociable, but also to put a picture frame around business conversations.** Engage in casual conversation before and after making a presentation to a client, selling a product, sharing an opportunity, negotiating a contract, providing a service, or conferencing with your child's teacher. A study conducted with physicians showed those who invest a few minutes asking patients about their families, their work, or summer plans, before or after an examination, are less likely to be sued than those who don't. Let's face it. People don't sue people they care about. And we are more likely to feel friendly toward people who show they care about us.

- **Express empathy.** Everyone is entitled to be listened to, even when in the wrong. Consider the client who sees the stock market rise 30 percent while his own portfolio doesn't. The stockbroker knows the client insisted on picking the stocks himself, but it would be a mistake to make the client "wrong." It's better to say, "I realize it's frustrating to experience this. Let's talk about what we can do from here." That goes a long way to diffusing negative emotions and helping the client feel friendly toward you—rather than tempted to move on to another stockbroker.

- **Acknowledge people warmly, make eye contact, and smile.** Again, be the first to say hello. If you don't you might be viewed as a snob. People often go back to their favorite restaurants because the hosts greet them with sincere smiles, look at them directly, and welcome them with warmth. My husband and I go to our favorite restaurant—and bring our friends there too—because the servers, the host or hostess, and even the owner take the time to help us feel extra special.

- **Use the other person's name in conversation.** You are more likely to get special treatment by using the other person's name. When you call to clarify a credit card billing, for example, when the person says his or her name, write it down. Then use it as you talk, finishing by saying, "Joe, thanks for taking the time to help me with this question." That helps Joe feel his role is important. If you don't know someone's name, take a moment to ask, and then repeat it. Be sure to pronounce it correctly. And, again, never presume your conversational partner has a nickname. As I shared before, my name is Debra, not Debbie. I don't like it when someone calls me Debbie. It's a little thing, but it's very important.

- **Show an interest in others.** In response to our high-tech environment of emails, voicemails, and faxes, we need high-touch more than ever. That's what you create when you show an interest in the lives of your prospects, customers, clients, associates, patients, or others whenever you have the opportunity to do so.

- **Dig deeper.** When you engage in a conversation, don't leave it too quickly. If your conversational partner mentions his or her vacation, pick up on the cue and dig deeper. Ask where that person went, what he or she did, what the highlight was, and if that person would go back. You'll help him or her feel better about you, as well as being glad about having spent the time with you. Always follow up with a question like "How's work?" or "What's been going on at work since the last time we spoke?" This way he or she knows you really want to hear about what is going on with the work part of his or her life.

- **Be a good listener.** This means making eye contact and responding with verbal cues to show you hear what the speaker says and are interested in hearing more. Verbal cues include phrases like: "Tell me more," "What happened first?," "What happened next?," "That must have been challenging," and so on. Making statements and asking questions like these lets people know you are actively listening to them.

- **Stop being an advisor.** If you mention a situation you are having with someone, do people offer advice without asking any questions? Have you ever put together a resume where someone told you it was too long, too short, too detailed, or not detailed enough? Giving unsolicited advice often irritates the recipient. Instead of advice, show understanding with simple phrases like: "I know you can work out a solution," or "I hope the job hunt goes well for you." Offer advice only when you are specifically asked for it.

An example I use in my presentations really makes the point about the *feel-friendly factor*. I wanted to find a good print shop near my home and walked into one near the busiest post office in our state. I was greeted with a sign that read: "Lack of preparation on your part does not constitute an emergency on our part." I asked myself, with that kind of a message, how many people would zip right into this shop for a few photocopies before mailing off an important package? I doubt that anyone would feel welcomed with the unfriendly attitude that sign reflects.

I then visited a printing shop across the street. Two colorful signs posted there made my day. One featured a cactus and said, "Stuck? We'll help you out of a prickly situation." The other showing a pot of jam read: "In a jam? We'll help you out of a sticky situation." You can guess which printer encouraged me to feel better about forming a business relationship.

Whether you want to land a new job, enhance your practice, gain listings, increase your billable hours, gain new clients or customers, bring new people into your business, or encourage people to remember you with referrals—pay attention to the *feel-friendly factor*. Then enjoy the success that follows.

"I strongly advise against using aggressive conversational tactics to get your point across. However, I do recommend using gently assertive rather than passive language. Your words need to convey your core strengths as well as your position."

—Debra Fine

-13-

Crank Up Your Conversational Clout with More Clarity

"Words help to tell your conversational partner where you stand and give clues about your attitude, confidence, and conviction."
—Debra Fine—

I strongly advise against using aggressive conversational tactics to get your point across. However, I do recommend using gently assertive rather than passive language. Your words need to convey your core strengths as well as your position.

Have you ever spoken words that are meek, apologetic, or hesitant? For example, when someone says, "I'll try to get back to you tomorrow," that person is really telling their conversational partner that under no circumstances will that happen! Try never makes anything happen. It's just a common excuse for being non-committal. You're either committed to getting back to the person or you're not.

The words we use in our conversations can convey messages we don't intend to deliver on. For example, has a member of the wait staff of a restaurant ever told you that

"We can't make substitutions," or a customer service rep responded to your inquiry with "If I can find out...."? Certain expressions and statements, as well as questions, can lead the conversation down an unintended path, or maybe nowhere. Say what you mean and mean what you say.

Consider the following examples, and pay attention to how you project yourself in the course of your future conversations:

- **Don't say:** "When will that be ready?" (Put yourself in the driver's seat.)
  Instead say: "Will you please have that ready for me this Tuesday?

- **Don't say:** "I'd hate to direct you to the wrong store." (Hate to do what? Hate to make a mistake?)
  Instead say: "I don't know what store to direct you to." Or, "I believe you can find that product at _____."

- **Don't say:** "I was going to say that property taxes seem high" and "I would think that roses would require more sunshine that this space provides." (This qualifies what you are about to say. Either statement sounds cautious and timid.)
  Instead say: "I believe property taxes are high" or "From my experience, roses require more sunshine than is provided in this space."

- **Don't say:** "Can I interrupt you for a minute? Can I ask you a question?" (You already have!)
  Instead say: "I'm sorry to interrupt..." and then ask your question. If you are willing to interrupt someone when they are engaged, just ask the question.

- **Don't say:** "I'll have to ask someone about that...." (Who are you? No one?)
  Instead say: I'll be glad to check with accounting and get back to you."

- **Don't say:** I'll be honest with you, I had a great time!"
(Aren't you always honest? Are you qualifying this particular statement over others you have made?)
Instead say: "I had a great time!"

- **Don't say:** "Can you spell your name for me?" (Most of us know how to spell our names. No one needs to be asked if he or she knows how!)
Instead say: "Please spell your name for me."

- **Don't say:** "If I can find out...." (A low expectation is established when you use the words "if" or "maybe." Raise expectations. Instill confidence.)
Instead say: "I will look into this immediately and get back to you tomorrow, one way or the other."

- **Don't say:** "I'm only the...." (Everyone's role or job is important. This is demeaning to oneself. Define the capabilities and responsibilities for your particular area of expertise.)
Instead say: "My responsibilities are focused on Website development, but I will be happy to check with sales about your order."

- **Don't say:** "I can't meet with you this morning." (This projects an unwillingness to deliver the best possible outcome. Or it projects a burden. In either case, say what you can do, not what you cannot.)
Instead say: "I can be there by 3:00 this afternoon."

- **Don't say:** "I'll try to get this back to you this week." (Once again, the word "try" conveys the underlying message that you aren't dependable.)
Instead say: "I'll get it to you no later than next week." (Tell people what you will do. Never tell them what you hope to do, or say something just to please them for the moment.)

- **Don't say:** "I'll have to check with my husband" or "I'll have to check with my secretary." (These statements make it seem like a burden to you.)
  Instead say: "I'll be happy to check with my husband" or "I'll be happy to speak to my secretary and get back to you."

- **Don't say:** "You'll have to call me tomorrow. This is a busy time for me." (This sounds like a person giving orders and placing another burden on my already heavy load! And no one likes to be bossed around.)
  Instead say: "You can call me tomorrow. That's a better time for me."

- **Don't say:** "I'm really not too sure." (Yes, you are! You are sure you don't know.)
  Instead say: "I don't know how to get to Colfax. Ask Jennifer. She's good with directions."

- **Don't say:** "May I ask your name?" (Permission is not necessary to ask someone's name!)
  Instead say: "My name is _____? What is yours?"

What we say is vitally important in our communications with others. Words tell your conversational partner where you stand and help convey your attitude, confidence, and conviction. Let your words communicate your strength and leadership.

"What we say is vitally important in our communications with others. Words tell your conversational partner where you stand and help convey your attitude, confidence, and conviction. Let your words communicate your strength and leadership."

—Debra Fine

"Take your life and business or career to a whole new level by diligently developing the power of meeting new people that's inside of you. You'll soon be growing in ways you haven't yet imagined, while dramatically accelerating your success."

—Debra Fine

-14-

Carpe Diem— Seize the Day!

"You'll soon be ready to chat comfortably
with people you don't know."
—Debra Fine—

A s we wrap up our discussion on meeting new people and having casual conversations, I am reminded of the professor in *The Wizard of Oz*, after his wizardry is discovered to be hocus-pocus. The erstwhile wizard gives a provocative monologue when he tells the Lion, the Tin Man, and the Scarecrow that they already have what it is they've been seeking. All they need to do to be courageous, have a heart, or be intelligent is to claim their own skills. The Wizard merely bestows his good wishes formally.

You now have all my trade secrets right here. I have no more magic or power than you. You only need to continue practicing the skills, tips, and techniques demonstrated in this book. So, without further ado, I ceremoniously honor your newfound skills:

By the power vested in me as a former nerd who lurked in the corners when she wasn't avoiding functions, who has transformed herself into a longtime successful meeter of new people and casual conversationalist, I do hereby confer upon you the title of *New People Meeter and Casual Conversationalist Extraordinaire.* As such, you are accorded all the rights, privileges, and responsibilities herewith. Let no party, gathering, group, or person intimidate you or squelch your efforts in meeting new people and casually conversing with them.

You are officially declared as a competent new people meeter and conversationalist. Let go of any old labels you may have given yourself that stand in the way of claiming those abilities as strengths of yours. The tips and approaches enumerated throughout the book are common-sense solutions to everyday people-meeting and casual conversation dilemmas. There is simply one requirement essential to achieving excellence at it—*doing it!*

Over and over again, I get confirmation about the value of meeting new people and having casual conversational skills. I love hearing about people whose lives have changed as dramatically as mine.

For example, a shy man in Florida got up the courage to ask a woman on a date, and now they're happily married. A quiet woman in Ohio got promoted to head up the entire Midwest region for her company. A gentleman in his 50s in Colorado is building a new life after his wife died of cancer. She had always done most of the talking for both of them, and now he can converse as well as the best conversationalists around.

Keep on going, even if you run into challenges. As Winston Churchill said, "This is no time for ease and comfort. It is the time to dare and endure." Practice with your family and friends first and, as you gain confidence, move on to business associates and other people you regularly see.

You'll soon be ready to meet and chat more comfortably with people you don't yet know.

Put yourself in social situations more frequently. Accept invitations. Join a trade organization, a volunteer group, or a club. At work, volunteer for projects that will allow you to associate with new and different people. Outside of work, go to events like boat shows, car shows, air shows, home shows, or any other situation where people are and introduce yourself to a new person. Casual conversational opportunities abound—especially when you find yourself with people you don't know who share a similar passion or occupation. During the next few weeks and months from now, review the following "Developing the Power of Meeting New People" worksheet: Compare your progress to your initial responses on page 13 now that you've implemented what you've learned in this book.

Developing the Power of Meeting New People

Check Yes or No to the following statements:

1. I have joined or participated in at least one club, group, or other activity in order to meet new people for business or personal reasons. ___ Yes ___ No

2. I'm conscious of taking turns in conversations so I can get to know others and help them get to know me. ___ Yes ___ No

3. I have helped at least two people meet potential associates, customers, or clients in order to assist them in their networking skills. ___ Yes ___ No

4. I have attended at least two functions, events, or activities a month where I can meet people who are either decision makers or potential new friends. ___ Yes ___ No

5. If someone is friendly toward me it is easy to be friendly back. However, I don't wait to make sure someone is friendly before I am friendly toward him or her. I initiate the friendly gesture. ___ Yes ___ No

6. When someone asks me "What's new?" instead of saying "Not much," I talk about something exciting.
 ___ Yes ___ No

7. At meetings, parties, and virtually everywhere I go, I introduce myself to people I don't know and come away knowing the names and having the contact information of at least three people. ___ Yes ___ No

Take your life and business or career to a whole new level by diligently developing the power of meeting new people that's inside of you. You'll soon be growing in ways you haven't yet imagined, while dramatically accelerating your success.

Who Is Debra Fine?

Debra Fine is the founder and owner of a company focused on teaching professionals conversational skills for use at networking events, conventions, and with prospects and clients. She is a former engineer and nationally recognized as a keynote speaker and trainer. Debra brings humor, as described in a *Denver Post* article, as a "mixture of stand-up comic, therapist, and teacher." Debra lives in Colorado with her husband Steve.

NOTES

NOTES

NOTES

NOTES

NOTES